Leathercrafting DIY

32 Timeless Projects ✚ Techniques

PIGPONG (Yoko Ganaha & Piggy Tsujioka)

SCHIFFER
PUBLISHING

4880 Lower Valley Road · Atglen, PA 19310

Contents

Introduction   4
About Tanned Leather   10
Purchasing Leather   12
Basic Tools   14
Basic Procedures   16

Chapter 1   18
Simple Structures

Card Case   20
Simple Smartphone Holder   20
Simple Document Case   22
Notebook Cover   24
Earphone and Cord Case   26
Mask Bag   28
Medicine and Bandage Case   30
Cases for Cosmetics and
   Candy   31
Envelope-Shaped
   Document Holder   32
Simple Clutch Bag   34
Zipper Pouch and Pen Case   36
Tall Tote Bag   38
Boxy-Bottom Shoulder Bag   40
Box-Shaped Clutch Bag   42
Box-Shaped USB, Pen, and
   Business Card Cases   44
Box-Shaped Smartphone
Holder   45
Pouch with Darts   46
Glasses and Accessory Case   48
Boxed-Corner Small Pouch   49
Plastic Bottle Holder   50

Chapter 2   52
Types of Leather •
Dyeing • Decorating •
Attaching Metal Fittings

Various Types of Tanned Leather 54
Dyeing with Liquid Dye   56
Indigo Dye on Leather   58
Dyeing with Paste   62
Dyeing with Markers   66
Edge Dyeing   68
Rubber Stamping   69
Embossing   70
Stenciling   71
Stitch on Flesh-Side and Turn
   Inside-Out   72
Thread Thickness and
Finishing   74
Special Stitching Methods   75
Metal Fittings   76
About Metal Fitting Positions 83
Buckles and Straps   84

Chapter 3   86
Intermediate-Level Structures

Binoculars Case   88
Bottom-Gusset Clutch Bag   90
Bicolor Tote Bag   92
Round-Bottom Shoulder Bag   96
Small Bag with Handles   100
Round Bag   102
Square Bag   104
Satchel-Style Bag   108
Drawstring Bag   112

Leathercrafting procedures are here. Refer to this chapter as you work on your project.

Chapter 4   114
Leathercrafting Basics

Preparing the Patterns   116
Rough Cutting   118
Transferring Patterns   119
Punching Stitching Holes   120
Cutting   122
Burnishing the Flesh-Side   124
Burnishing Edges   125
Gluing Leather   126
Preparing Thread and
    Needle   128
Begin Stitching   129
Saddle Stitch   130
Running Stitch   131
Ending Stitching and
    Dealing with Thread Ends   132
Stitching Steps   134
Finishing   135

All the project patterns!

Chapter 5   136
Patterns

INTRODUCTION   About This Book

This book presents methods for easily making a large number of designs AND for expanding upon their variations by taking advantage of characteristics unique to Tanned Leather.

Leathercrafting Is Actually Quite Easy

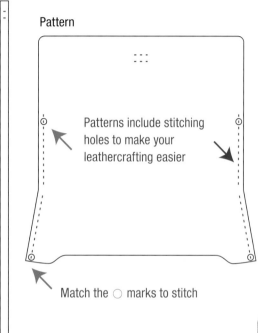

Pattern

Patterns include stitching holes to make your leathercrafting easier

Match the ○ marks to stitch

HOW TO

You can make items just by cutting according to the pattern and sewing the pieces together.
It's very similar to paper crafting, where glued edges are pressed together.
When making bags with fabric you need special knowledge, such as folding seam allowances to prevent fraying, inserting stabilizers to firm up bags, and adding linings. With leather, though, you can just cut and stitch. That's perfectly fine!
Patterns in this book contain hole positions for each stitch.
For hand-sewn leather, be sure to make your stitching holes before sewing.
Properly punching stitching holes is the most important part of hand sewing.
If the number of holes is correct, you can just sew along the holes and you're done!

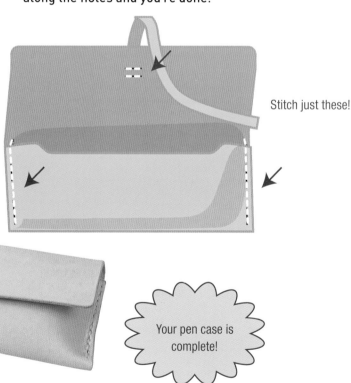

Stitch just these!

Your pen case is complete!

Leather Can Be Molded as Needed

Tanned leather is stiff, so when you finish sewing it might look like you've just sewn some cardboard together. But don't worry, you can still manipulate its shape dramatically.

If you moisten with water, fold...

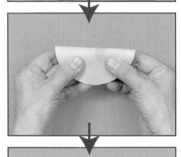

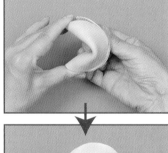

and then let it dry, the leather will "remember" its shape.

Leather Fortune Cookie

See Chapter 5 for instructions.

See Chapter 5 for instructions.

Thin leather can be softened by simply applying leather oil, or by rubbing it in with your hand. In addition, thin leather can be sewn like cloth.

Changing the shape

At first the leather is just sewn flat together. But, once moistened, a slim round container can be pressed in and then the leather will dry and that shape will remain.

Grain-sides facing each other, stitch together. Then, turn the grain-side out.

5

Leather Changes over Time

Tanned leather changes to a beautiful amber color through friction and caused by daily use.

AGED This symbol appears on projects when leather has already gone through the aging process.

Leather Changes over Time

Aging can be sped up by leaving the item on a windowsill for a few days.

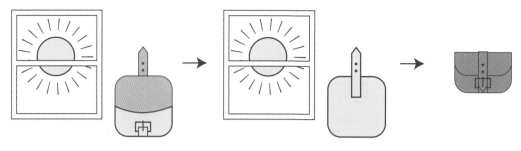

Leave in a sunny area for 2 to 3 days. Leave flap open.

Turn over and flip around so tanning is even. Repeat, while applying leather oil.

One special characteristic of tanned leather is that it wears in as you use it or manipulate it. For example, if you rub the leather forcefully with your hands, little by little it will begin to soften. Replenishing the leather oil will add to the suppleness.

The pale, grain-side surface turns a lovely amber color as you use the leather product. Through frequent rubbing and exposing to sunlight, your leather products begin to look as though they were crafted many years ago.

Conversely, if you want to keep the original look and feel of the leather longer, be sure to keep it out of direct sunlight when not in use. You can even put it in a cloth, and leave it in a cabinet or drawer. Just be careful not to forcefully stuff too many items in the bag or it may deform.

To Finish with a Beautiful Amber Color

As with human skin, leather can become damaged when exposed to very strong summer sun or heat. Always treat your leather with the same care as your skin. Slowly exposing to gentle sunlight is the key to not causing damage.

Add leather oil to a soft cloth and then thinly, and carefully, apply it to the leather to prevent drying. If applied diligently every two days or so, the leather will break in nicely. Be sure not to apply too much. If you do add a lot, it will not be absorbed and you'll just end up with an uneven finish.

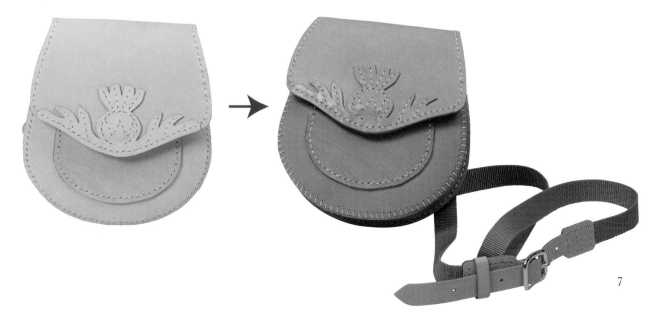

You Can Dye Leather or Add Decorations

Stamps, stencils, dyeing, indigo dyeing, painting, etc.: Tanned leather, especially natural vegetable tanned, is well-suited for these types of embellishment. Methods are explained in Chapter 2. Note that throughout this book we've omitted any decoration from the how-to photos and images, to keep the instructions easy to understand. Be creative and have fun!

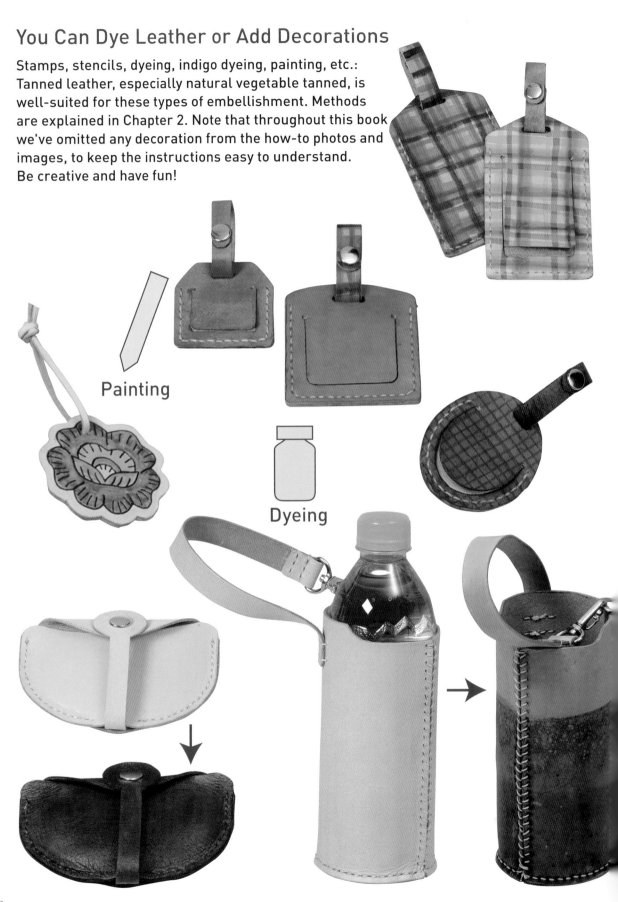

Painting

Dyeing

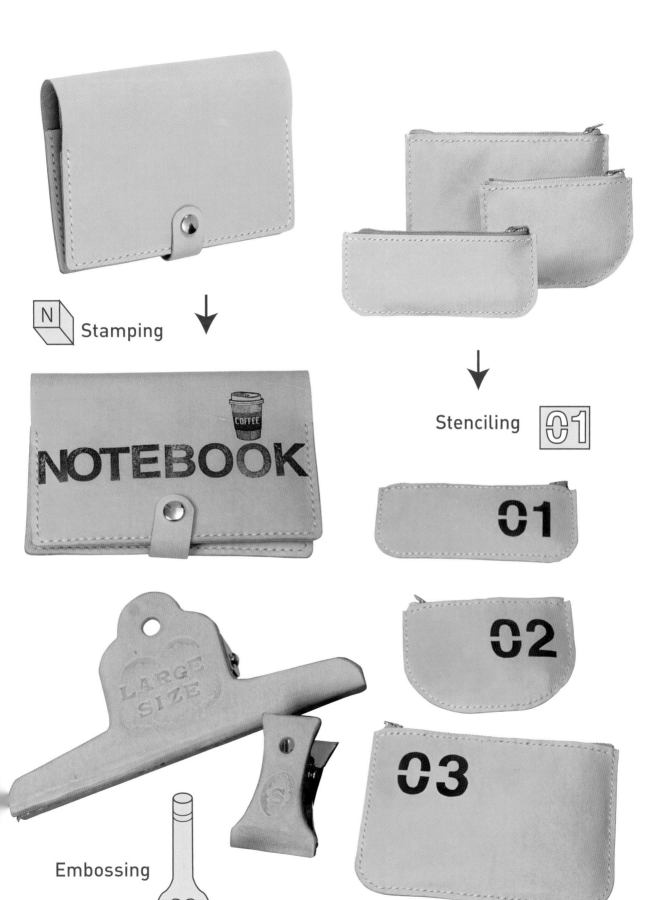

Stamping

Stenciling

NOTEBOOK

COFFEE

01

02

03

Embossing

LARGE SIZE

9

ABOUT TANNED LEATHER

In this book, "natural vegetable tanned leather" will simply
be referred to as "tanned leather," while "oil-tanned
leather" will be explicitly labeled as such.

Tanned Leather Is...

The "skin" of any animal will rot if left as-is.
"Leather" is an animal hide that has been tanned for preservation. Common methods include vegetable
(tannin) tanning and chrome tanning.

Tannins are natural substances – some are found in black tea, some in trees, fruits, vegetables, etc.
Vegetable (tannin) tanning, which has been around for a very long time, is the term for a method that uses
chemicals contained in tree bark.
Due to the primitive nature of this process, it is very time-consuming.
The various broadly termed "vegetable tanned leathers" are simply called "tanned leathers."
If worn-out vegetable tanned leather is simply thrown away it will gradually decompose into soil, similar to
what happens with dead animals in the wilderness.

Chrome tanning is a tanning method that uses chemical agents.
Since it takes fewer steps than vegetable tanning, and since it can be industrialized, most commercially
made leather products are chrome tanned. This leather is often dyed or has some surface finishing.

Generally, leather tanned with tannins is called "tanned leather." But, in the narrow sense, only leather that
has been tanned naturally, without being processed, may be correctly called "tanned leather."

[Natural Vegetable Tanned Leather]
This is vegetable tanned leather that is used for dyeing.
It is the most popular leather for crafting because it has less oil and is therefore easier to dye.
The natural vegetable tanned leather is durable and firm and has a pinkish cream color.

However, it has some negative characteristics: the surface is easily scratched, it tends to absorb moisture,
it is easily stretched when wet, and the color changes easily due to oxidization.

That being said, it is easy to work with and to form shapes with this type of leather. In addition, it becomes
soft, and more lustrous, when broken in. It changes shades gradually to a nice warm, amber color. Which is
to say, natural vegetable tanned leather embodies the authentic feel of broken-in leather.

Since natural vegetable tanned leather is not treated with any surface finishing, there are areas that contain
scars, bug bites are clearly visible, and wrinkles and veins show up.
Of course, this all just reflects the fact that the leather is an authentic animal skin.

If we don't view those little imperfections as flaws, we can enjoy working with this leather's qualities, and
enjoy using our very own leathercrafted bags and everyday items.

[Part Names]

In leathercrafting, the front side is called the "grain-side," the rear side is called the "flesh-side," and the cut side is the "edge."

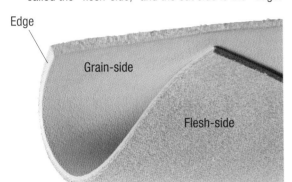

Edge

Grain-side

Flesh-side

The grain-side of natural vegetable tanned leather is easily dented, even with just a little pressure.
Even pressing on the grain-side with a fingernail can leave marks.

Pre-waxed hand-stitching thread easily collects impurities.
So, removing excess wax is recommended. To do this simply rub the thread between two pieces of cloth.
Since natural vegetable tanned leather is generally low in oil, supplementing with leather oil is recommended after you complete your work. This makes the leather last longer.

You can specify thickness when purchasing leather.
This book uses relatively thin, 1.8 mm, 1.4 mm, or 1 mm ($1/16$ in.) leather.

[Oil-tanned leather]

Although tanned, this type of leather is softer than natural vegetable tanned leather because it is suffused with a healthy amount of oil. Similar to natural vegetable tanned leather, oil-tanned leather is suitable for making hand-stitched leather products. In addition, production steps are the same for both types of leather.

Dyed leather for crafting is also available. If you want to make something with a particular color we recommend that you use "oil-tanned leather" as it will be more evenly dyed than any hand-dyed pieces.

The main advantage of dyed leather is that it hides scratches, color variations, sunburn, etc. In other words, it's more worry free.

It is safe to apply Leather Lacquer Finish to colored leather before sewing. This will prevent color transfer and stop the color from being rubbed off. If you want to use a dark colored piece and a light colored piece in the same project, be sure to wet the edge of the leather and test for color transfer with a piece of paper towel. Avoid using them together if you find any transfer.

PURCHASING   Purchasing Leather

Leather can be purchased at specialty stores of course, but you can also find it at major arts and crafts supply stores.

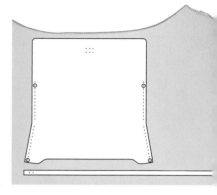

When purchasing off-the-shelf leather, be sure to bring the necessary full-scale patterns and arrange them on the leather in order to make sure it is large enough. Even though the pattern includes seam allowances, I would recommend choosing leather that is larger than what is needed in order to compensate for cutting margins, bends in the leather, stretching, etc.

Leather from different parts of the animal displays different characteristics. How the pattern is placed on the leather and how each item is cut becomes very important. If there are damaged areas, or areas that can be easily stretched, check to see that they are usable or if it is possible to avoid these areas completely.

As far as metal fittings go, there are many varieties available.
There may be times when it's hard to decide which metal fittings to use, and which tool goes with which fittings.
When choosing leather and metal fittings it's always a good idea to confirm with a knowledgeable expert at the shop or supplier.

[Leather Measurement Units]
Each hide has a unique shape.
Sometimes "ds" is used as a unit of measurement.
1 ds is 10 cm squared (approx. 4 in. squared).
A ds measures how many 10 cm squared (approx. 4 in. squared) sections will fit in a rectangular shaped piece of hide.

**1 ds =
10 x 10 cm (approx. 4 x 4 in.)**

[Selecting Leather]

Spine Side

Half Cowhide

Cow leather, seen here, comes in halves that are tanned.

Belly Side

Make sure there are no branding marks or scars on the area you intend to use.
If there are, be inventive – for example, if you are making a bag, hide the branding/scar by covering it with a pocket, etc.

Do not use the areas marked with slanting lines to make the body of a bag or 1-ply handles, as these areas have uneven thickness and are prone to stretching. The slant-lined areas are most appropriate for making small, 2-ply items. When using remnant leather, place your patterns so that you avoid areas that will wrinkle (like those marked with slanting lines).

Uneven Finish
Aging will lessen conspicuous differences in color, but avoid extreme differences if possible.

Leather from the area marked with slanted lines
Bags will be distorted with this leather because it stretches easily, especially in the direction of the grain.

Flesh-side is coarse
If the flesh-side is whitish and/or fluffy in comparison to other areas, it is likely to produce wrinkles.

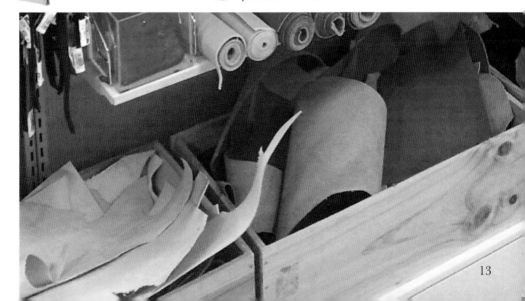

13

TOOLS Basic Tools

Other setting tools are listed in "Attaching Metal
Fittings" pp. 76 ~ 81.

Gluing/Attaching patterns

Glue Stick
Use glue with low water content to keep the
pattern from wrinkling.

Drafting Tape

To temporarily secure
patterns, use drafting tape
that can be easily removed
from the grain-side of the
leather.

Gluing Leather

Adhesive
Use a type of adhesive that requires application
on both surfaces.
Apply the adhesive and bond the leather together
by applying pressure until the adhesive has dried.

Burnishing

Tokonole (Tragacanth
substitute)
Apply when burnishing the
flesh-side or edge of the
leather.

Wood Slicker
Used for slicking areas where Tokonole has
been applied.

Dresser
A file used to adjust and polish edges.

Cutting Leather

Vinyl Board
A thick vinyl mat.
Place under the leather when cutting.

Large Utility Knife
Use for cutting the leather.

Punching Stitching Holes

Lacing Chisels

Instructions given in this book use 1 to 1.8 mm / ¹⁄₁₆ in. thickness tanned leather and a 5mm / ¼ in. wide, four-prong lacing chisel. The stitching holes marked on the patterns are set for 5mm / ¼ in. wide, four-prong lacing chisel as well. If you use a different size lacing chisel, the stitching hole intervals will not match with the marks on the pattern, so be aware.

Use four-prong chisels for straight lines and two-prong chisels for curved lines. The picture shows prong width (actual size). Different shapes are available for the shaft.

mm / ¼ in.   5mm / ¼ in.

Scratch Awl
Use this for marking positions or scoring lines.

Single-hole Punch
Used for punching round holes. Various sizes are available.

Lacing Needle
Used for punching individual stitching holes.

Wooden Mallet
Use this for striking the lacing chisel and the hole punch.

Rubber Plate
Place this under the leather when punching holes, etc.

Stitching

Unwaxed Linen Thread
Manually apply wax before stitching.

Double-Waxed Thread
Polyester double-waxed thread.

Wax Block
Wax for arts and craft use.

Leather Needles
The tip is slightly round.

Finishing

Leather oil
Superior absorbent leather care oil. Use soft fabric and apply thinly. Thoroughly coat the leather surface.

Leather Lacquer Finish
A finishing agent that has superior water-resistance and anti-friction effect. Used to seal dyes and for finishing after dyeing.

HOW TO: Basic Procedures

This production flow applies to all projects in this book.
Chapter 4, "Leathercrafting Basics," provides details for each task.
Carefully read Chapter 4 prior to beginning your project.

Preparing Patterns P116

Rough Cutting P118

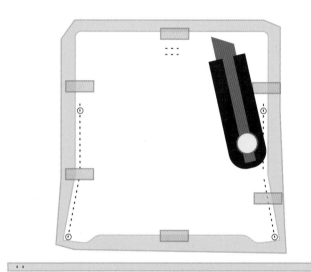

Cutting P122

Burnishing the Flesh-Side and Edges P124

The flowchart uses the Basic
Pen Case as an example.

Transferring Patterns P119 >

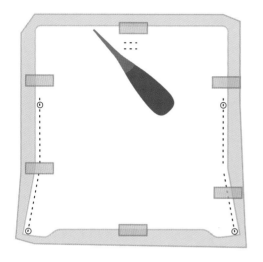

Punching Stitching Holes P120 >

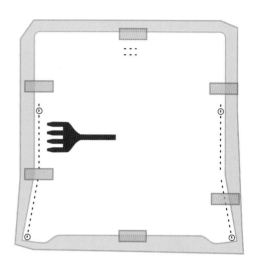

Gluing and then Stitching P126~132 >

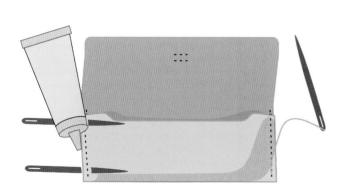

Finishing P134 >

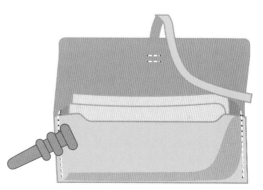

CHAPTER 1

Simple Structures

A great way to start is by making a simple structure, with few parts, from this chapter.

Item sizes vary, but projects with similar patterns and leathercrafting methods are introduced in order.

Even the larger items are surprisingly easy if you understand the reasoning behind them.

Refer to Chapter 4, "Leathercrafting Basics."

The "HOW TO" section from Chapter 1 teaches the methods.

★ Confirm the number of stitches and their positions on the pattern provided.

★ The figures used in the "HOW TO" sections are small, so the gluing method and beginning sewing positions are simplified. Be sure to use the procedures in Chapter 4.

★ The finishing process is omitted here. See p. 136.

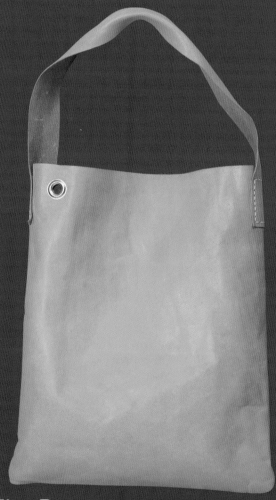

pattern

Join 2 pieces

Flat Bag

Leather thickness = 1.8 mm / 1/16 in.   AGED

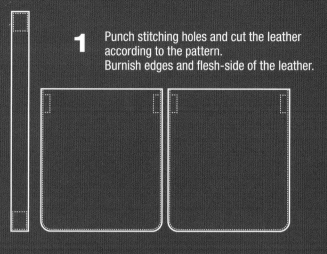

1 Punch stitching holes and cut the leather according to the pattern.
Burnish edges and flesh-side of the leather.

2 Grain-sides facing each other, align the stitching holes, glue then stitch. Refer to p. 72.

Confirm the number of stitches, and their positions, on the pattern provided.

See p. 126 for gluing. Confirm the stitching start position on p. 129.

Make small incisions at the corners.

3 Turn the grain-side out.

4 Attach the handles.
Refer to the pattern and align the stitching holes. Then, glue and stitch.
Attach a grommet before stitching if you want one on the finished product.
Refer to p. 77.

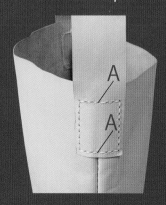

A

A

pattern

Stitch layers together

Card Case • Simple Smartphone Holder

Leather thickness = 1.8 mm / $\frac{1}{16}$ in. Oil-tanned leather and tanned leather

Bus pass/business card and mobile phone case. This is a simple structure that you just sew together.

HOW TO:

[Card Case]

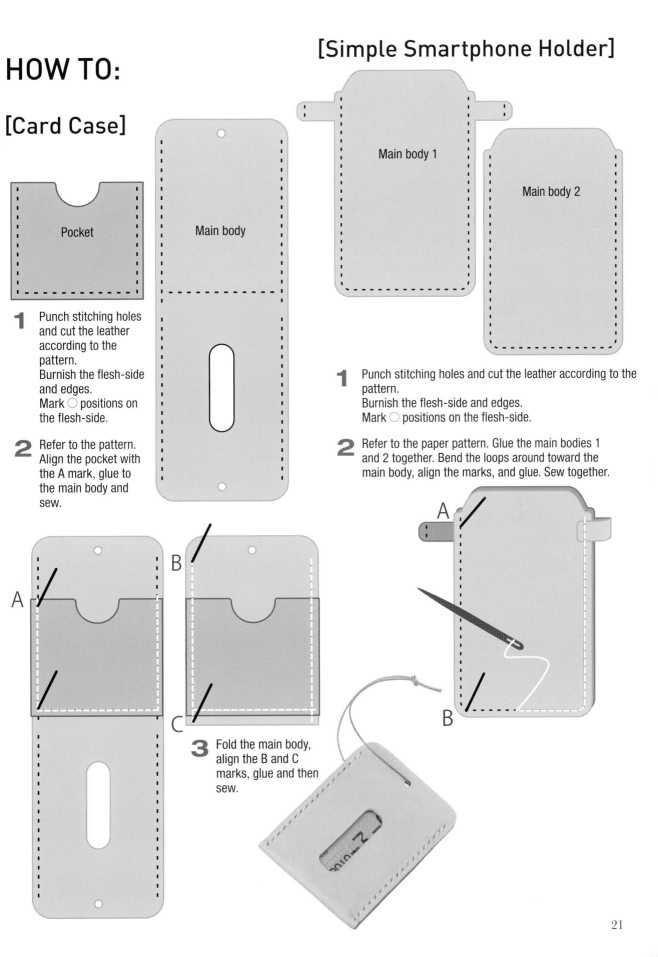

Pocket

Main body

1 Punch stitching holes and cut the leather according to the pattern.
Burnish the flesh-side and edges.
Mark ○ positions on the flesh-side.

2 Refer to the pattern. Align the pocket with the A mark, glue to the main body and sew.

[Simple Smartphone Holder]

Main body 1

Main body 2

1 Punch stitching holes and cut the leather according to the pattern.
Burnish the flesh-side and edges.
Mark ○ positions on the flesh-side.

2 Refer to the paper pattern. Glue the main bodies 1 and 2 together. Bend the loops around toward the main body, align the marks, and glue. Sew together.

A

B

A

B

C

3 Fold the main body, align the B and C marks, glue and then sew.

21

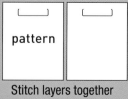

pattern

Stitch layers together

Simple Document Case Leather thickness = 1.8 mm / 1/16 in. `AGED`

A thick, solid leather document case that can hold heavy items. It is quite easy to make because you just have to sew two pieces together.

HOW TO:

Main body

1 Cut two pieces of leather according to the pattern. Punch the stitching holes. Burnish the flesh-side and edges. Mark ○ positions on the flesh-side.

2 Align the two corners and marks while referencing the pattern. Glue and sew.

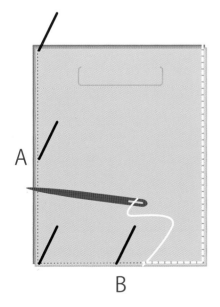

A

B

Before folding to make the handle.
Before aging.

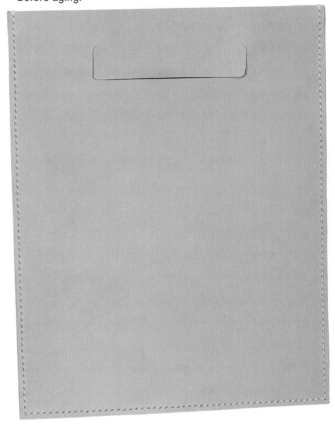

For the handle holes, simply moisten and fold inward.

pattern

Notebook Cover Leather thickness = 1.4 mm / 1/16 in.

A notebook cover that is just the right size for notebooks and postcards. This size holds items measuring 105 x 148 mm / 4⅛ x 5⅞ inches.

HOW TO:

1 Punch stitching holes and cut the leather according to the pattern.
Burnish the flesh-side and edges.
Mark ○ positions on the flesh-side.

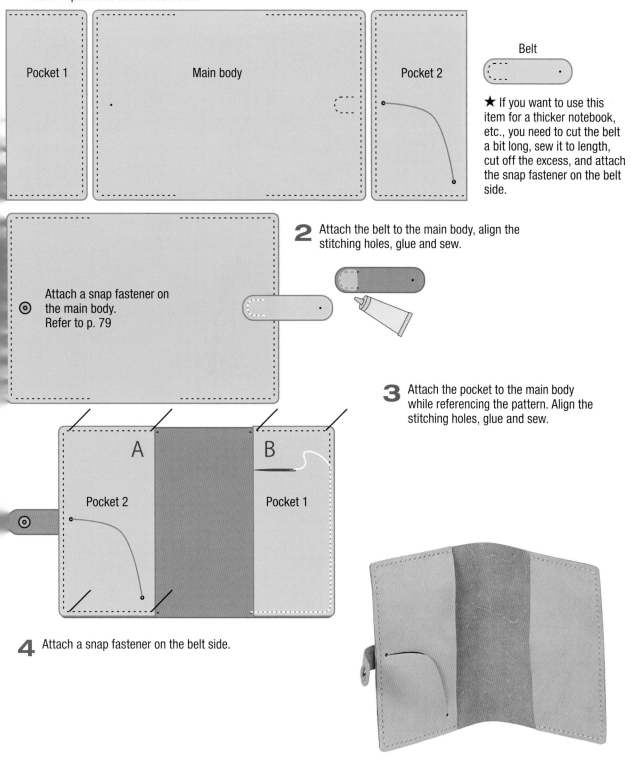

Pocket 1

Main body

Pocket 2

Belt

★ If you want to use this item for a thicker notebook, etc., you need to cut the belt a bit long, sew it to length, cut off the excess, and attach the snap fastener on the belt side.

⊙ Attach a snap fastener on the main body.
Refer to p. 79

2 Attach the belt to the main body, align the stitching holes, glue and sew.

3 Attach the pocket to the main body while referencing the pattern. Align the stitching holes, glue and sew.

A

B

Pocket 2

Pocket 1

4 Attach a snap fastener on the belt side.

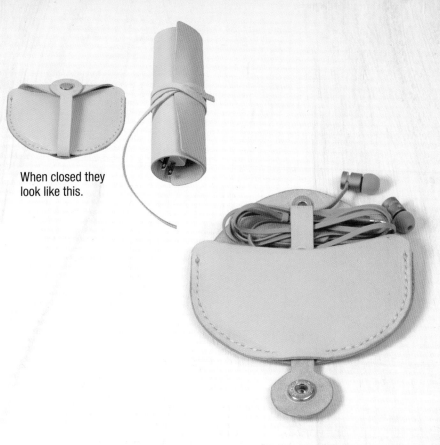

When closed they look like this.

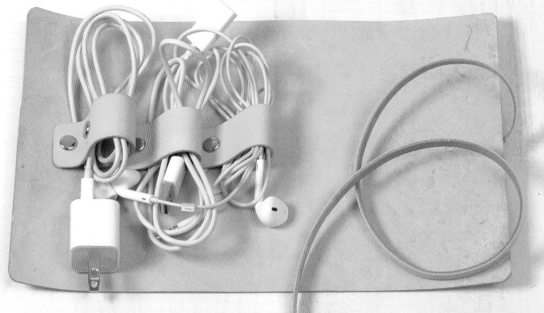

pattern

pattern

Join 2 pieces

Single piece

Earphone and Cord Case Leather thickness = 1.8 mm / $\frac{1}{16}$ in.

The belt inside snugly holds earphones. After storing cords by fastening them with the inner belt, roll up the case to close.

HOW TO:

[Earphone Case]

1 Punch stitching holes and cut the leather according to the pattern. Burnish the flesh-side and edges. Mark ○ positions on the flesh-side.

Belt

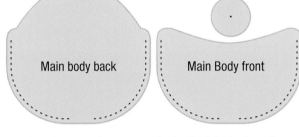

Main body back

Main Body front

2 Attach a snap fastener on the back of the body and one end of the belt.

Refer to p. 79.

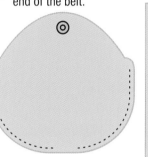

3 Align marks on the back and front of the main body, glue them together, and sew.

4 Thread the belt and attach a snap fastener to the other side of it.

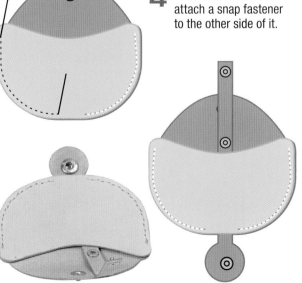

[Cord Case]

Main body

Belt (long)

String

Belt (short)

1 Punch stitching holes and cut the leather according to the pattern. Burnish the flesh-side and edges.

2 Attach a snap fastener on each belt.
Attach 2 snap fasteners to the long belt so the thickness can be adjusted.

3 Attach each snap fastener to the body.
Align the stitching holes, glue and sew.

4 Glue the string to the main body by aligning the stitching holes and sew.

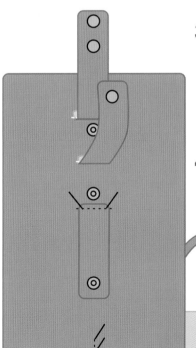

27

Backside of the bag

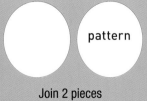

pattern

Join 2 pieces

Mask Bag Leather thickness = 1.8 mm / $1/16$ in. Oil-tanned leather and tanned leather

A playful abstract mask image makes this bag special. Applique
tanned leather on dyed leather.

HOW TO:

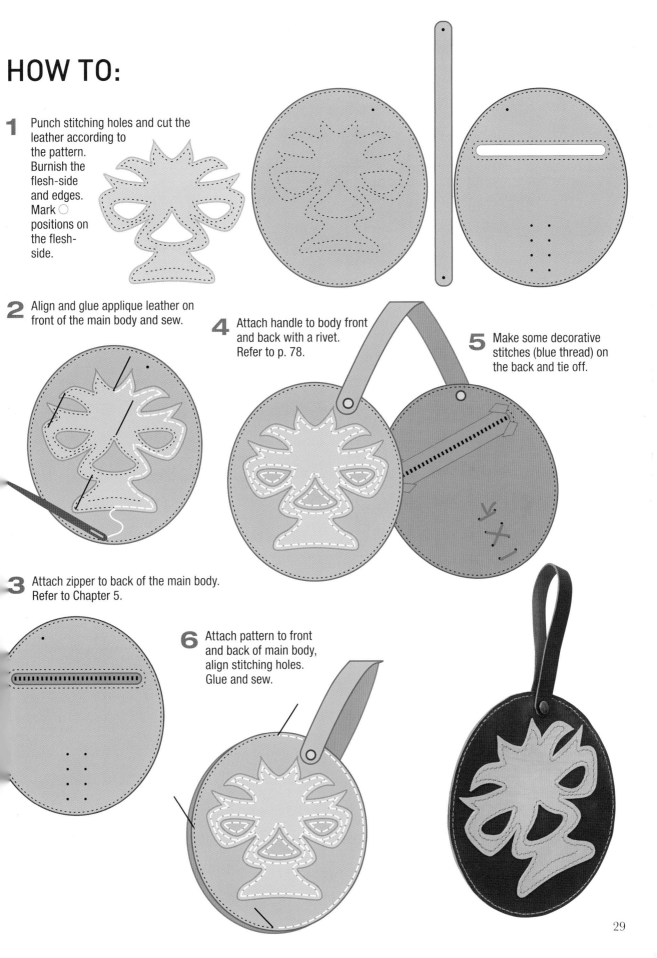

1 Punch stitching holes and cut the leather according to the pattern. Burnish the flesh-side and edges. Mark ○ positions on the flesh-side.

2 Align and glue applique leather on front of the main body and sew.

3 Attach zipper to back of the main body. Refer to Chapter 5.

4 Attach handle to body front and back with a rivet. Refer to p. 78.

5 Make some decorative stitches (blue thread) on the back and tie off.

6 Attach pattern to front and back of main body, align stitching holes. Glue and sew.

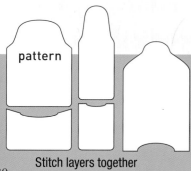

pattern

Stitch layers together

Medicine and Bandage Case

Leather thickness = 1.8 mm / $^1/_{16}$ in. Oil-tanned leather and tanned leather

This type uses the belt or notch to easily fasten the flap.

■ See Chapter 5 for instructions.

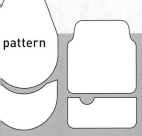

pattern

Stitch layers together

Cases for Cosmetics and Candy

Leather thickness = 1.8 mm / $1/16$ in. Oil-tanned leather and tanned leather

Simply sew two pieces of leather, one on top of the other. Lightly moisten and add something that is slightly thick. Then allow to dry. Your item will assume that shape. Leathercrafting is fun!

■ See Chapter 5 for instructions.

pattern

Join 2 pieces

Envelope-Shaped Document Holder

Leather thickness = 1.8 mm / $\frac{1}{16}$ in.

A bag where the flap is secured with a string. It's like an envelope for storing documents.
The leather is thin, so it will become soft and broken in with use.

HOW TO:

String stopper pieces

Make each string stopper 2-ply by adding a second leather piece, gluing, and then punching holes. Refer to p. 127.

1 Punch stitching holes and cut leather according to the pattern.
Burnish the flesh-side and edges.
Mark ○ positions on the flesh-side.

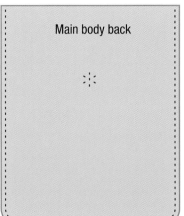

Main body back

Main body front

3 Align stitching holes and sew front and back of main body while referencing pattern.

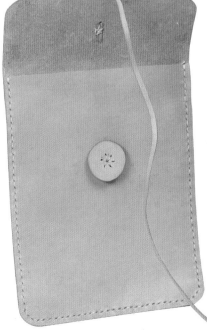

2 Align stitching holes and sew string stopper on front and back of main body. Do not glue the stopper pieces.

Pass string through to back of main body. Sew over the string on the flesh-side. Glue tip.

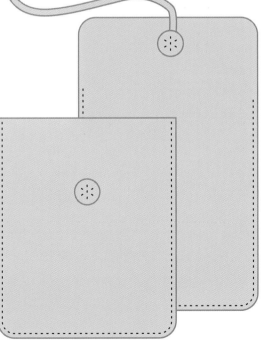

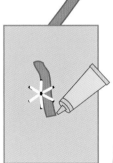

pattern

Join 2 pieces

Simple Clutch Bag Leather thickness = 1.8 mm / ¹⁄₁₆ in. `AGED`

This is just two pieces of leather sewn together, but it makes a really solid bag. We need fairly large pieces for the main body, so the flap is made from a separate piece.

HOW TO:

1 Cut leather according to the pattern and punch stitching holes.
Burnish the flesh-side and edges.
Mark ○ positions on the flesh-side.

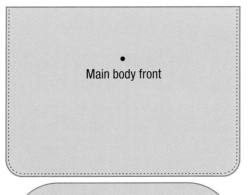

Main body front

Flap

Main body back

2 Attach Sam Browne stud to front of main body.
Refer to p. 81.

3 Align stitching holes, while referencing the pattern, and glue flap to back of main body. Sew.

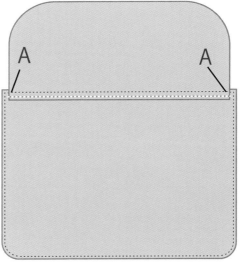

A   A

A

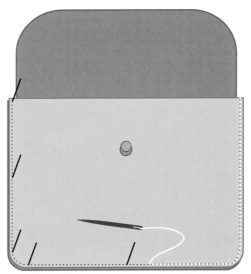

4 Align stitching holes of main unit, glue and sew.

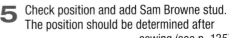

5 Check position and add Sam Browne stud. The position should be determined after sewing (see p. 135) and testing size by adding items to clutch.
Refer to p. 81.

★ For this piece make two holes with a slit between them so size can be adjusted.

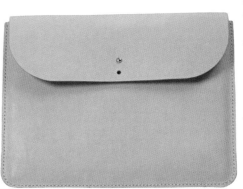

pattern

Bottom is folded

Zipper Pouch and Pen Case
Leather thickness = 1.8 mm / $\frac{1}{16}$ in.

Pouch and pen cases that open and close with a zipper. Bottom is folded to make a gusset.
The method is the same for both items.

HOW TO:

[Pen Case]

1 Punch stitching holes and cut leather according to the pattern. Burnish the flesh-side and edges. Mark ○ positions on the flesh-side.

Leather pieces for zipper pull tabs

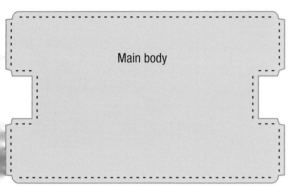

Main body

2 Attach zipper. See Chapter 5.

3 Overlap both side seam allowances. Align stitching holes, glue and sew.

★ If you use 1mm / 1/16 in. leather and the same pattern and then stitch the grain-sides facing together, you will get this result.
Refer to p. 72.

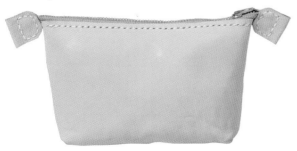

5 Apply glue to zipper pull tabs.

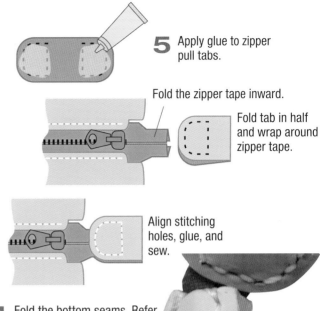

Fold the zipper tape inward.

Fold tab in half and wrap around zipper tape.

Align stitching holes, glue, and sew.

4 Fold the bottom seams. Refer to pattern and glue seam allowance together. Begin stitching.
(Photograph shows Zipper Pouch)

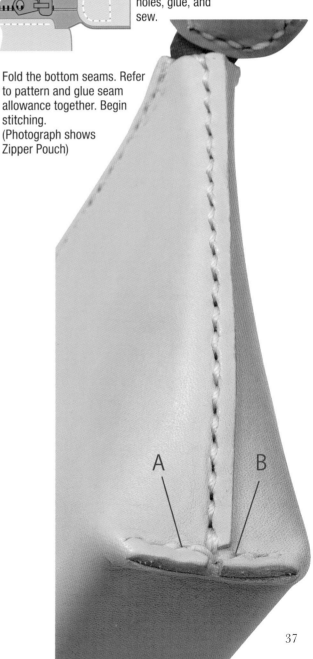

A

B

pattern

Folded bottom

Tall Tote Bag Leather thickness = 1.8 mm / 1/16 in. AGED

This is a gusseted tote, folded along the bottom. However, it is sewn inside out with thin leather and then reversed, thus producing a gentle finish with less visible stitching.

HOW TO:

1 Punch stitching holes and cut leather according to the pattern.
Burnish the flesh-side and edges.
Mark ○ positions on the flesh-side.

Main body

Handle

2 Apply glue on the handles, along the seam allowance. Fold in half lengthwise, align stitching holes, and glue according to pattern. Sew to position A.

A

A A

A A

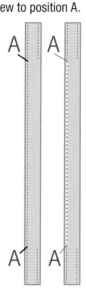

3 Glue handle to main body while aligning stitching holes. Sew.

A

4 Fold with grain-side in. Glue sides together while aligning stitching holes. Sew.
Reference pattern. Glue bottom while aligning stitching holes, B to B and C to C. Sew.

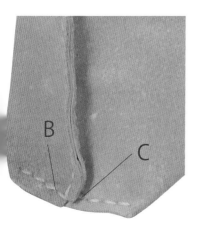

B

C

5 Turn the grain-side out. Refer to p. 72.

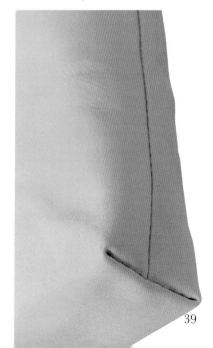

pattern

Folded bottom

Boxy-Bottom Shoulder Bag Leather thickness = 1.8 mm / 1/16 in. `AGED`

The bottom is folded in at the ends, so the front side of the bag has a trapezoid shape. To counter this, the sides of the bag narrow toward the opening.

■ See Chapter 5 (p. 156-158) for instructions.

detail

pattern

Assemble a
box shape

Box-Shaped Clutch Bag Leather thickness = 1.8 mm / 1/16 in. `AGED`

Bend leather at right angles, just as you would when making a paper box, and
sew. This particular bag is quite large, but smaller items (see following pages)
can be made in the same way.

HOW TO:

1 Punch stitching holes and cut leather according to the pattern.
Burnish the flesh-side and edges.
Mark ○ positions on the flesh-side.

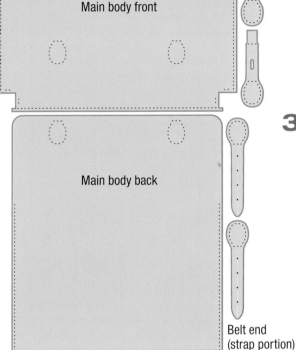

Main body front

Belt buckle piece

Main body back

Belt end (strap portion)

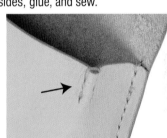

Main body back

Main body front

2

C   **1**   C

3 Put front and back sides together. Refer to pattern.
1 Glue the bottom seam as you align the stitching holes. Then sew. Moisten the leather and fold the bottom corners in tightly. Fold seam allowance toward grain-side.
2 Now align stitching holes on the sides, glue, and sew.

4 Moisten and pinch the top corners of front panel. Sew along stitching holes.

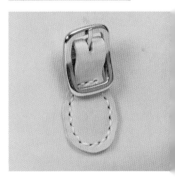

2 Glue belt buckle piece to front of main body, and belt end to the back. Be sure to properly align all stitching holes. Then, sew.
Refer to p. 84.

Belt buckle piece

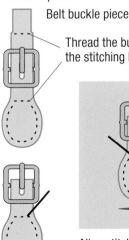

Thread the buckle, fold it, align the stitching holes and glue.

Align stitching holes with those on main body front, glue, and then sew.

Belt end (strap portion)

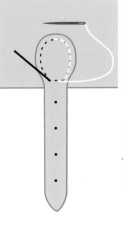

5

Align stitching holes on bottom corners of main body front and sew.

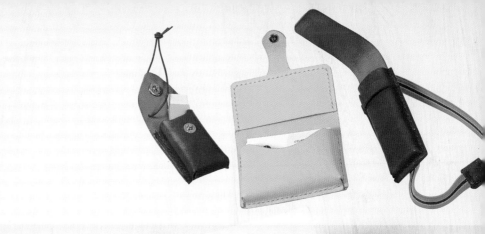

pattern

Assemble a box shape

Box-Shaped USB · Pen · Business Card Cas

Leather thickness = 1.8 mm / $1/16$ in. Oil-tanned leather and tanned leather

This small USB case, pencil case, and business card case each have th same structure as the bag on p. 42.

■ See Chapter 5 for instructions.

Assemble a box shape

Box-Shaped Smartphone Holder

Leather thickness = 1.8 mm / ¹/₁₆ in. Oil-tanned leather and tanned leather

The red case has a Sam Browne stud closure and belt loop. The tanned leather case has a fold-over flap and a strap to hang it from another bag, etc.

■ See Chapter 5 for instructions.

pattern

Dart on bottom
corners

Pouch with Darts Leather thickness = 1.4 mm / 1/16 in. `AGED`

Notches sewn together produce this lovely bag with darts.
Rounded gussets, created through the use of darts, produce a softer effect.

HOW TO:

1 Punch stitching holes and cut leather according to pattern. Burnish the flesh-side and edges.
Mark ○ positions on the flesh-side.

Reinforcing pieces

Main body front

Main body back

Glue

Glue and sew

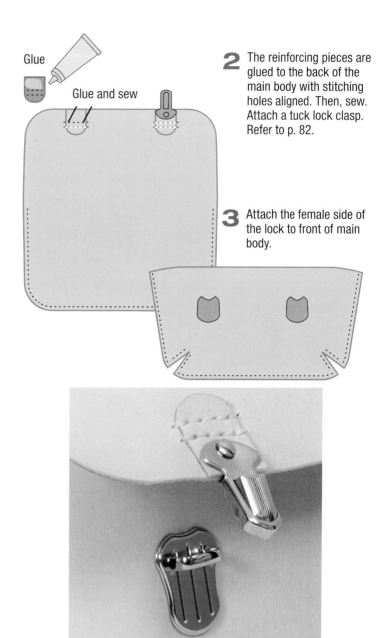

2 The reinforcing pieces are glued to the back of the main body with stitching holes aligned. Then, sew. Attach a tuck lock clasp. Refer to p. 82.

3 Attach the female side of the lock to front of main body.

4 Sew darts on front of main body by aligning their edges and cross-stitching. See p. 75.

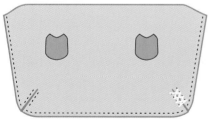

5 Glue front and back of main body together while referencing the pattern. Be sure to properly align A, B, and C. Sew.

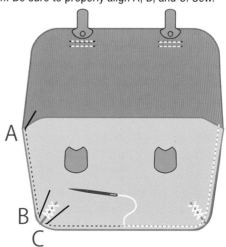

A

B

C

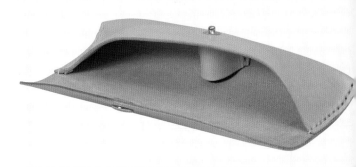

pattern

Odd-shaped pattern

Glasses and Accessory Case

Leather thickness = 1.8 mm / $\frac{1}{16}$ in.

These pieces are made from a single, folded piece of leather. But, if they are just sewn along the stitching holes the accessory case might be too plump.

■ See Chapter 5 for instructions.

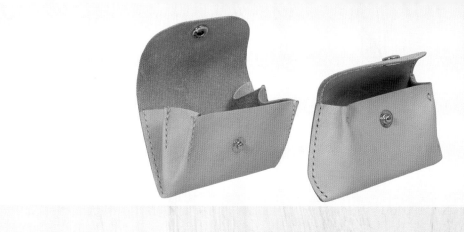

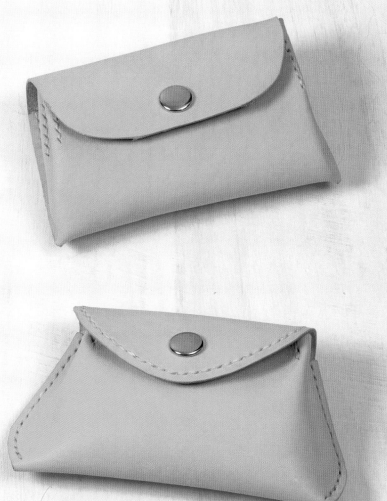

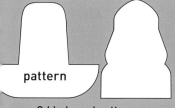

pattern

Odd-shaped pattern

Boxed-Corner Small Pouch

Leather thickness = 1.8 mm / $\frac{1}{16}$ in.

These are altered versions of the previous page. The extra leather is gathered together and bulges at the sides.

■ See Chapter 5 for instructions.

pattern

Odd-shaped pattern

Plastic Bottle Holder Leather thickness = 1.8 mm / $\frac{1}{16}$ in. AGED

Made from a unique pattern with a round bottom. Matching up the stitching holes is easier when the pattern doesn't have separate side and bottom pieces. The sides are sewn like a baseball so the seam is flat.

HOW TO:

1 Punch stitching holes and cut the leather according to the pattern. Burnish the flesh-side and edges. Mark ○ positions on the flesh-side.

Strap

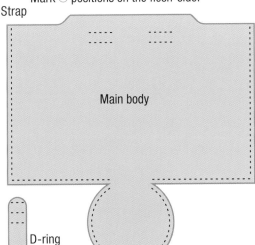

Main body

D-ring leather piece

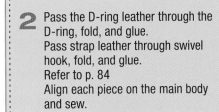

2 Pass the D-ring leather through the D-ring, fold, and glue.
Pass strap leather through swivel hook, fold, and glue.
Refer to p. 84
Align each piece on the main body and sew.

4 Moisten the bottom and fold inward toward grain-side. While referencing the pattern, align, glue, and sew along stitching holes.

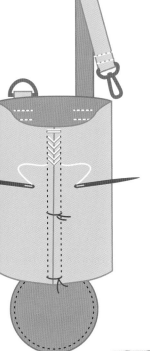

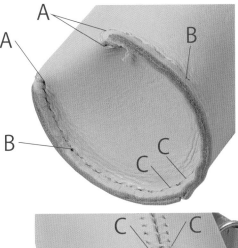

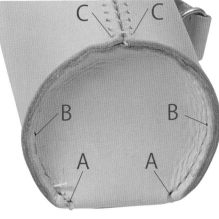

3

Align the edges of the main body and line up the stitching holes. Temporarily fasten with threads in several places (shown in red). Baseball stitching Refer to p. 75.

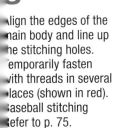

CHAPTER 2

Types of Leather
Dyeing
Decorating
Attaching Metal Fittings

Tanned leather offers a variety of methods for creating
original designs. Here we'll look at some of the most common.
Remember that you can also come up with your own!

Metal fittings, dyes, finishes, and more are ways to alter the feel
of your finished leather project.

When using any products on your leather, always read and
follow their instructions carefully.

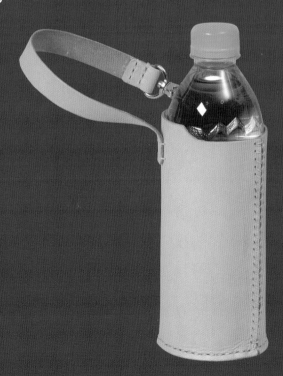

Various Types of Tanned Leather

Cow, calf, and other animals

All made from the same pattern. Look closely at the different "expressions" of each type of leather.

Each item has a different texture and softness, but they are all attractive.

The projects in this book are varied, but also offer plenty of ways to let your creativity flow. There are items that have beautiful fasteners, those where the stitching is not visible, and even those that don't have any metal fittings whatsoever, like locks or Sam Browne studs. Be sure to challenge yourself and have fun!

■ See Chapter 5 for instructions.

Tanned Cow Leather

1.8 mm / 1/16 in. thickness

This is the thin leather. This item was turned inside-out after sewing. Knead well, or soak in oil, to create a soft and supple finished product.

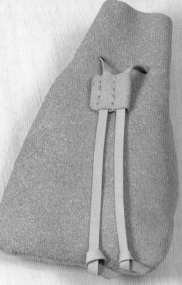

Tanned Cow Leather

1.8 mm / 1/16 in. thickness

This is a solid leather used for items in this book.
This type is a little thick for drawstring pouches, but as you use it, it will break in and become supple.

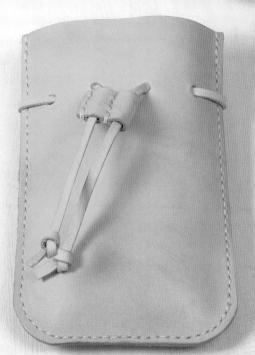

Tanned leather

1.8 mm / 1/16 in. thickness

With the flesh-side facing up. The flesh-side is a bit rough and some leather fibers might come off, but it produces an interesting look.

Tanned Deer Leather (Deerskin)

This is a very light and supple leather that is still durable and strong.

Tanned Sheep Leather (Sheepskin)

This is a soft and supple leather sometimes used in clothing.

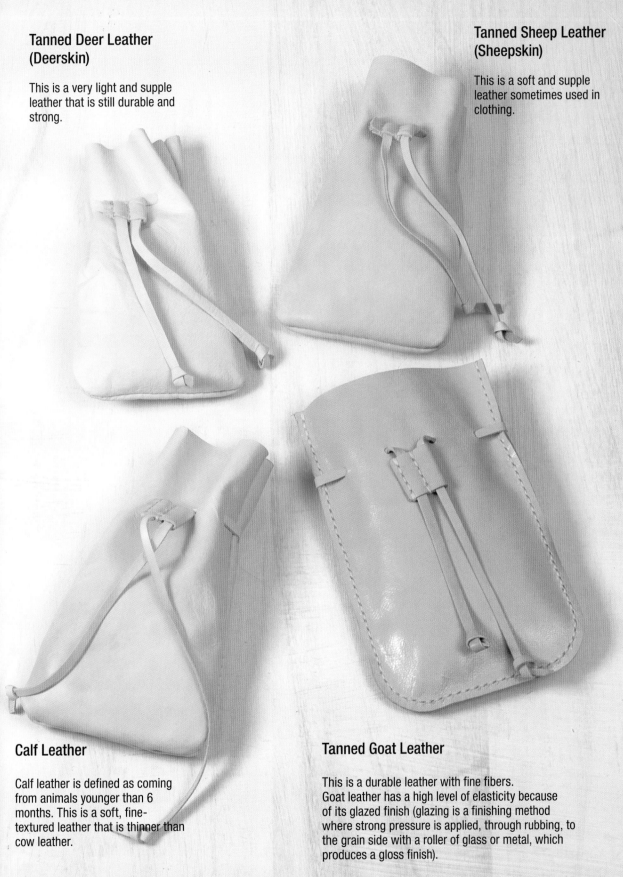

Calf Leather

Calf leather is defined as coming from animals younger than 6 months. This is a soft, fine-textured leather that is thinner than cow leather.

Tanned Goat Leather

This is a durable leather with fine fibers. Goat leather has a high level of elasticity because of its glazed finish (glazing is a finishing method where strong pressure is applied, through rubbing, to the grain side with a roller of glass or metal, which produces a gloss finish).

Dyeing with Liquid Dye

Among tanned leathers, "natural vegetable tanned leather" is best for dyeing because it's light in color and absorbs a lot of dye. It dyes bright too. Roughly cut leather can be dyed with liquid dye (before sewing). Note that it is difficult to evenly dye large surfaces, so dyeing is best reserved for smaller items.

A name tag made with dyed leather.
■ See Chapter 5 for instructions.

Dye

Roapas Batik (Batik Leather Dye)
A strong leather dye that produces good coloring.
It's easy to handle, can be diluted with water, and even mixed with other dyes.

★ When dyeing, lay down some vinyl or something similar so you won't stain your table. Be careful or your hands and clothes will get stained. Thoroughly wash all brushes and tools after use.

1 Dry leather absorbs dye quickly, so lightly moisten your piece to prevent uneven coloring. If you want your dyeing to be light, make sure your piece absorbs more water.

2 Put dye in a paper cup and apply with a brush. Apply so as not to have any gaps.

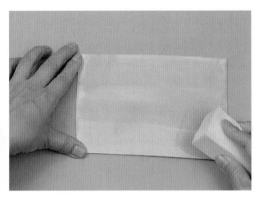

3 Apply evenly while changing direction from horizontal to vertical and back. Careful, if the leather becomes soaked with water it won't absorb the dye. If this happens just use a tissue to absorb the water and wait a bit before dyeing.

★ You can also draw patterns using different colors.

★ When applying to edges that have been cut, lightly soak a cotton swab, etc., in Tokonole and apply gently to the edge. That way the edge won't absorb too much dye.

★ After drying, apply Leather Lacquer Finish to complete. Leather oil can also be used, even though its coating power is inferior, as this will help retain the natural leather texture.

Leather Lacquer Finish

A water-based finishing agent with excellent water resistance and abrasion resistance. It can be used for everything from color fixing to finishing without changing the texture of the leather. Brush with the stock solution or dilute with water. Estimated dry time is 30 minutes. (One day for complete drying.)

Indigo Dye on Leather

The beautiful color produced by indigo dyeing has long been loved in Japanese society. More recently, the rest of world has caught up in appreciating it. The examples below, instead of being dyed uniformly, use a more rustic approach.

Two types of pen case. The one on top is a dyed version of the "Zipper Pen Case" from p. 36. The method for constructing the lower case can be found in Chapter 5.

Dye

Indigo Dye Kits

Indigo dye kits are widely available, like this one from Konya-I. Kits are an easy way to enjoy indigo dyeing.
* Surface-processed leather will not accept the dye.
* Chemical fibers (like polyester used for zippers, pull tabs, etc.) will not accept the dye.

[Before Use]

Color unevenness will tend to occur because the product is soaked and dyed. The intensity and specific indigo color you wish to have often can't be achieved. In addition, tannins in the leather can cause brown staining. So it's important to understand that indigo dyeing has a "natural" finish, meaning there will often be uneven coloring. Here, the cotton fabric of the zipper is also dyed.

If wax is used before dyeing, it will repel the indigo dye solution's moisture and not dye cleanly.
The sections coated with Tokonole are also dyed, but only lightly.

The water bottle case is dyed by dipping, so the inner flesh-side will also be dyed. Be aware that the leather fibers on the flesh-side may peel off and stick to anything you put inside, or may stain light-colored fabric. (You can improve this situation a little by applying Tokonole when finishing.)

Try to dye the flesh-side as little as possible. The flesh-side of the pen case with the zipper is a little hard to dye when the zipper is closed.

Along with the stress caused by the indigo dyeing, the leather will also be soaked once, all of which can cause damage. Also, note that 1.8 mm / 1/16 in. thick leather sides, bottoms, or straps can be easily cut. In addition, if you leave the item as-is after dyeing it will shrink. So, after dyeing, stuff a towel or other padding inside the item to reduce shrinkage.

Dyed "Plastic Bottle Holder" from p. 50.

1 Make indigo dye according to the instructions. Use unfinished and nonoiled leather pieces.

★ When dyeing, lay down some vinyl sheeting, etc. so the table doesn't get dirty. Be careful as your hands and clothes will stain. Wash all equipment thoroughly after use.

2 Gently place leather in the indigo dye and soak for about 10 seconds. Then remove and expose to air.

When indigo touches the air, it changes from green to blue. However, since leather contains water and has a slightly dark color, you have to intuit the finished dye color. So, before dyeing you should check the coloring by dyeing a small cut-off piece, or hidden section, of your item.

If it is too dark, just dilute with water before use. If you try it out and feel that the dye is too light, just repeat the process.

3 If you want your item to be "gradient dyed," just repeat step 2 from halfway down.

4 You can neutralize indigo by acidifying it. Add 20cc vinegar to 1 liter of water and mix well. Soak the dyed leather in the vinegar and water solution for one minute and then immediately, gently scrub with a sponge while holding it under running water.

5 Be sure to remove moisture from the washed leather.
Quickly stuff old towels inside the item and tightly wrap the outside in old towels as well. Press tightly so they absorb as much moisture as possible.

Once dried, apply leather oil and rub to soften.
Applying oil and rubbing for a few days will restore suppleness.

Be careful: if left without oil until completely dry the leather will become overly stiff. If you want to fix the dye in place, apply Leather Lacquer Finish ONE DAY after the oil.

Dyeing with Paste

This method can intentionally produce broken-in/ aged leather over time.

From the top. "Pouch with Darts," p. 46, and "Glasses and Accessory Case," p. 48.

Dye

Paste Dyes

A wax-type paste dye for leather spreads well. It is easy to apply and doesn't produce much unevenness. The examples we use here are: Carving Dye Antique is dark and used when you want to make your chosen leather deeper and darker.

Carving Dye Clear can be dyed and rusted at the same time. Concave sections will dye deeply. To prevent discoloration, apply Leather Lacquer Finish (or similar) to finished product.

Carving Dye Antique Usage   Carving Dye Clear Usage

Left is the "Earphone Case," p. 26. Right is the "Basic Pen Case," p. 115.

How to Produce Broken-In Leather That's Closer to the Images

Before dyeing, moisten and knead well to deform.

When using thick leather, it is best to stuff an old towel inside to prevent unnecessary wrinkles. Then go ahead and apply leather oil and knead. Once soft, remove the towel and knead again.

Before Dyeing

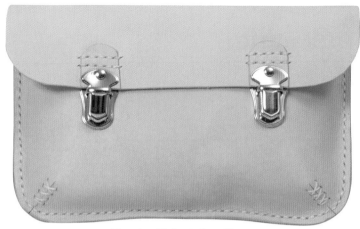

"Pouch with Darts," p. 46

1 Apply Carving Dye with a soft cloth once slightly moistened.

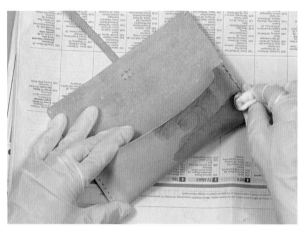

2 In order to produce a damaged feel, you can lightly file curved surfaces and "damage" the grain-side.

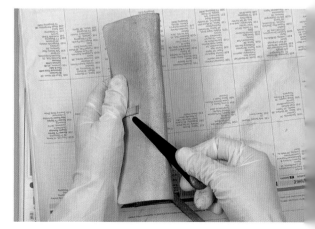

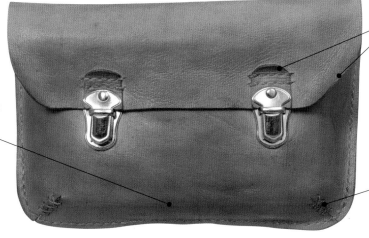

Stained

If you dye the flap while bending, it will have a more worn-in feel.

Lightly file the curved surface at the bottom and rub in some dye.

Firmly apply Carving Dye to the corners and seams. Rub to blend.

3 Apply plenty of Carving Dye to the filed part and rub.

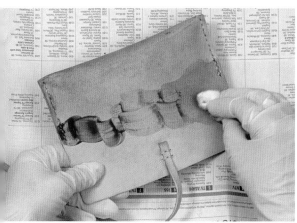

4 Rub Carving Dye on the edges.

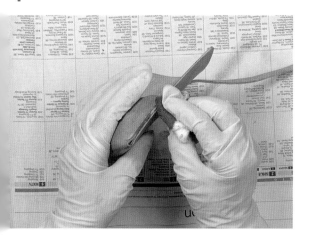

5 Repeatedly apply to areas you want to darken.

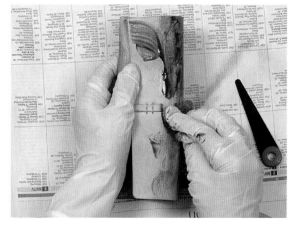

Dyeing with Markers

Marker pens can easily color small items and are available in a wide variety of colors.

■ See Chapter 5, "Dyeing with Markers" Charm.

1 Place a design on lightly moistened leather and tape it down with drafting tape. Trace the design using a ballpoint pen that has run out of ink while pressing down firmly.

2 The moistened grain-side of the leather is easily scarred, so the design will remain on the leather. The lines will remain after the leather dries.

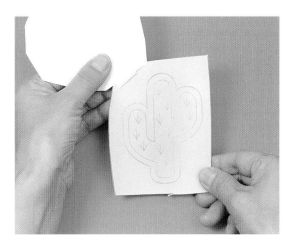

3 Once the leather dries, color with a fabric marker. When using multiple colors, be sure to go from light to dark.

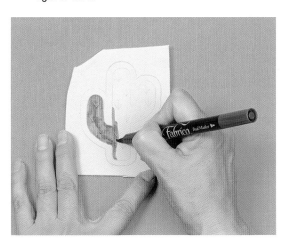

4 Outline the contours, and details, with a water-resistant ballpoint pen.

Ink ballpoint pens that become water resistant once dry

Fabrico Dual-Tip Fabric Marker

Aqueous pigment-based ink marker.
A marker that can draw on both fabric and leather. There is no need to coat the surface of the target piece.
If you use a blow dryer to apply warm air, the ink will fix more firmly. If you want to use a finishing agent after coloring, be sure to test it on a scrap piece of leather first.

Edge Dyeing

Edge colorants are rich in color and add a fun or contemporary touch. They are ideal for small items like key chains.

■ See Chapter 5, "Edge Dyeing" Key Chain.

Cova Super Edge Coat

An aqueous acrylic resin-based edge coloring finish. If you burnish the edge first and then apply, you will achieve a beautiful luster. This protects the edge from fading, even when wet.

Burnish edge with Tokonole. Apply Cova Super with toothpicks or disposable chopsticks. Cova Super Edge Coat is one of the available brands. A similar product is Eco-Flo Edgeflex Edge Paint. Please choose the product that is most available for you.

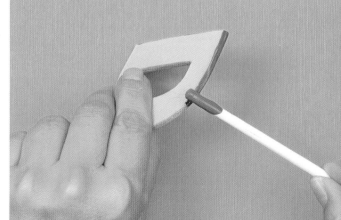

If you want to put a logo or pattern on your project, rubber stamps work well.

Faded stamps look great on tanned leather.

★ Rubber stamps can't be used well unless the leather is flat. Stamp before sewing whenever possible.

"Notebook Cover," p. 32, features stamping.

StazOn Multisurface Ink Pad

Stamp ink that works on leather.
Water resistant, so there is no need to coat the surface. Doesn't absorb color like with dyeing, so may come off through rubbing because it is just attached to the surface instead of penetrating it. If you want to apply oil or a finishing agent to the stamp it may fade, so be sure to test on a scrap piece before using.

If you want to align the top and bottom of the letters, you can use a book or box as a guide.

Embossing

Decorate with metal-stamping tools.

■ See Chapter 5, "Embossing" Clipboard.

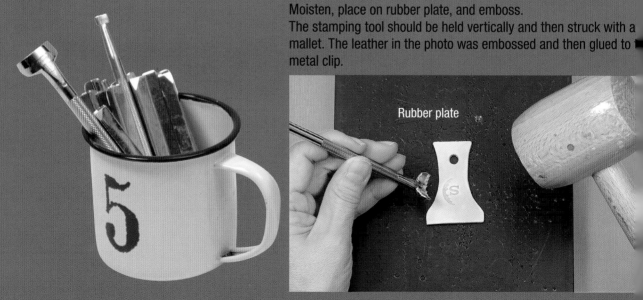

Moisten, place on rubber plate, and emboss.
The stamping tool should be held vertically and then struck with a mallet. The leather in the photo was embossed and then glued to metal clip.

Rubber plate

A stencil drawn on leather.

Paint Tex (or similar)

A resin pigment type paint.
One application will sufficiently dye an item.
The result is clear, similar to regular dye.

Doesn't absorb color like with dyeing, but may come off through rubbing because it is just attached to the surface instead of penetrating it.
Paint Tex is one brand available to use stenciling the leather. When it is difficult to find it in your area, Angelus Leather Paints can be used to achieve a similar effect.

★ Stencils are easier to apply to flat leather, so apply before sewing.

■ See Chapter 5, "Stenciling" Flat Pouch.

1

Make a stencil.
Place a sheet of clear plastic over the design and trace with an oil-based pen. Remove the design and cut out the stencil with a utility knife.
Be very careful when cutting.

2

Place on leather and attach with drafting tape so it won't shift.
Wad up some cloth to make a dabbing pad. Apply Paint Tex (or similar) to the pad, and lightly blend by first dabbing on some newspaper. Now apply by tapping the pad over the stencil and transferring the Paint Tex to the leather.

Stitch on Flesh-Side and Turn Inside-Out

This item was sewn with the flesh-side facing up.

■ See Chapter 5 for instructions.

Use thin leather, about 1.8 mm / $1/16$ in. thick. Enjoy that lovely feeling when firm or stiff leather becomes soft and supple.

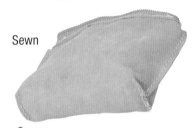

Sewn

★ If you apply Tokonole to the flesh-side, the leather will become even stiffer. So, it is best to sew first.

★ Be careful not to allow the glue to squeeze in from the seam allowance.

★ Thread a needle on just one end of the thread and use a running stitch as this leather is quite thin. Be careful not to pull the thread too tight.

If you make notches in the corner, it turns inside-out more easily.

1 Apply leather oil to the grain-side (inside).

2 Knead well to soften. Apply a thin coat of oil and knead. Repeat for a few days to make even softer.

3 Slowly and gently turn inside-out.

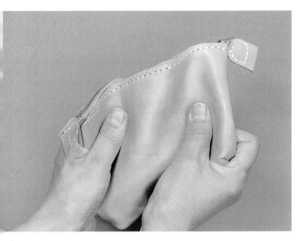

4 Apply leather oil again and knead well.
It is better to apply the leather oil little by little over several days, rather than all at once.

5 Once soft, apply Tokonole to the flesh-side.

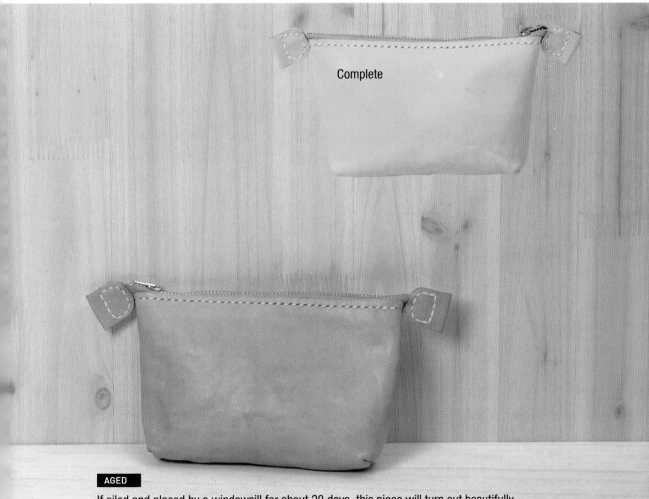

Complete

AGED

If oiled and placed by a windowsill for about 20 days, this piece will turn out beautifully (photo above).

★ When turning inside-out, wrinkles may remain depending on the part and its thickness.

Thread Thickness and Finishing

Linen thread for hand-sewn leather.
To be waxed before use.
There are numerous diameters of thread.
Choose according to the look you wish to create.
Medium-fine thread is used throughout this book.

Thick

Medium-fine

Thin

Thick

Medium-fine

Thin

Butt Stitch
Sewing with needles on one end

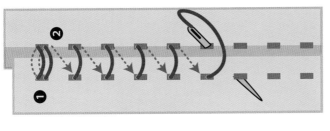

1 Pass the thread from the first stitching hole to the one across from it. Do this twice.

2 Pass the needle diagonally underneath the leather and push out stitching hole down and adjacent to the entry point.

Baseball Stitch
Sewing with needles on both ends

Temporary Stitch

Match the edges up and sew. For items with really long seams, it is best to temporarily fasten them in several places.

1 Pass the thread from the first stitching hole to the one across from it. Do this twice.

2 Pass the needle diagonally behind the leather to the hole down and across from the entry hole. Advance the left and right needles at the same rate and pull the thread evenly.

★ The length of the thread is about 7 times the sewing distance.

★ If you sew so that either the left or right thread is always on top, you will get a much cleaner seam.

Cross-Stitch
Sewing with needles on both ends

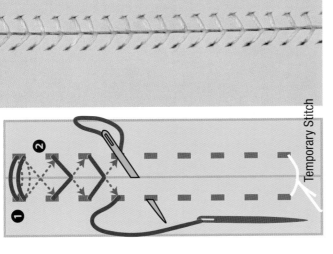

Temporary Stitch

Match the edges and sew. For items with really long seams, it is best to temporarily fasten them in several places.

1 Pass the thread from the first stitching hole to the one across from it. Do this twice.

2 Pull the needle through and then move down and across diagonally.

3 Pass the needle through to the adjacent hole under the leather. Advance the left and right needles one step at a time and pull evenly.

★ The length of the thread is about 7 times the sewing distance.

★ If you sew so that either the left or right thread is always on top, you will get a much cleaner seam.

Metal Fittings

This section introduces methods for attaching metal fittings used in leathercrafting, such as rivets and snap fasteners.

This book shows the basic versions, but there are various types of magnet clasps and catch tuck locks.

Be sure to position the single-hole punch and setter perpendicular to the leather when punching.

Be sure to practice on some end pieces since metal fittings cannot be redone.

Punching Holes

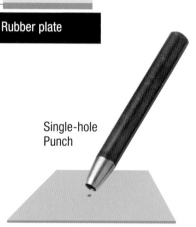

Single-hole Punch

Leather

Grain-side

Rubber plate

A single-hole punch is used to cleanly punch rounded holes.
There are various sizes. Punching is almost always performed on the grain-side.

Single-hole Punch

1 Line the single-hole punch up with the mark.

2 Line up the single-hole punch vertically and firmly strike with a mallet.

Single-hole punch size chart

Use this as a guide when making holes for lacing and metal fittings. Hole sizes are actual size.

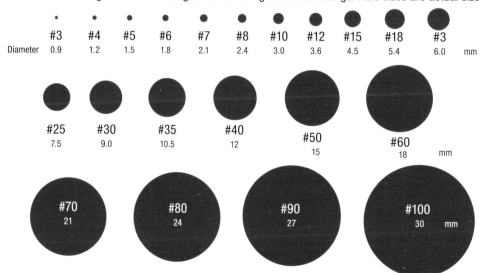

	#3	#4	#5	#6	#7	#8	#10	#12	#15	#18	#3	
Diameter	0.9	1.2	1.5	1.8	2.1	2.4	3.0	3.6	4.5	5.4	6.0	mm

#25	#30	#35	#40	#50	#60	
7.5	9.0	10.5	12	15	18	mm

#70	#80	#90	#100	
21	24	27	30	mm

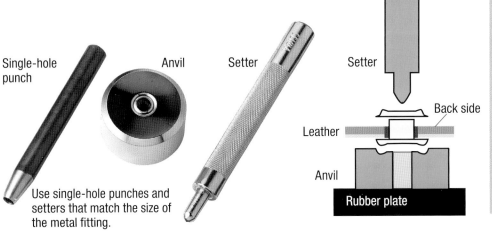

Single-hole punch

Anvil

Setter

Setter

Back side

Leather

Anvil

Rubber plate

Use single-hole punches and setters that match the size of the metal fitting.

Grommet

1

Place the piece with the barrel in the groove of the anvil.

2

Place perforated leather, flesh-side up, over the barrel. Then, add washer portion of grommet.

3

Stand setter vertically over the washer and strike with a mallet. Tilting can be adjusted by striking the setter while rotating little by little.

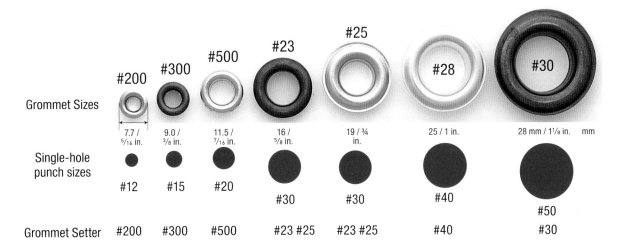

	#200	#300	#500	#23	#25	#28	#30
Grommet Sizes	7.7 / ⁵⁄₁₆ in.	9.0 / ³⁄₈ in.	11.5 / ⁷⁄₁₆ in.	16 / ⁵⁄₈ in.	19 / ¾ in.	25 / 1 in.	28 mm / 1¹⁄₈ in. mm
Single-hole punch sizes	#12	#15	#20	#30	#30	#40	#50
Grommet Setter	#200	#300	#500	#23 #25	#23 #25	#40	#30

Rivets

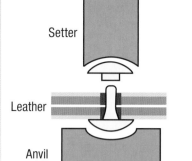

Setter

Leather

Anvil

Rubber plate

Post sizes vary.
When employing thick
leather, longer than usual
posts are needed.

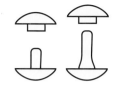

If the cap is flat, use
a completely flat
setting base.

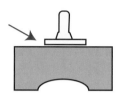

Used for attaching
two or more pieces of
leather.

Choose the correct size of
single-hole punch and rivet
setter based on the size of
rivet you intend to use.

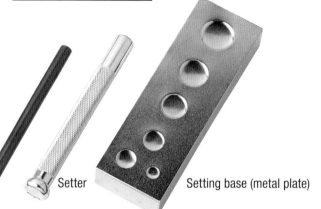

Single-hole punch   Setter   Setting base (metal plate)

Extra Large

Setter Size: Extra Large

Short po

12.5mm /
1/2 in.

●
#10

Long po

Large

Setter Size: Large

Short p

9mm / 3/8 in.

●
#8

Long po

Small

Setter Size: Small

Short p

6mm / 1/4 in.

●
#7

Long po

1 Match the rivet post with the
appropriate hole in the setting base.

2 Cover with perforated leather. Add the
cap portion of the post.

Setter Size: Extra Small

Short p

4.6mm / 3/16 in.

3 Make sure the post and setting
base are properly aligned. Strike
the vertically stabilized setter with a
mallet.

#6

Single-hole punch size   ●

No. 8050 Extra Large

Setter Size: 8050

Cap side

A   B

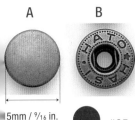

15mm / ⁹⁄₁₆ in.

 #25

Post side

C   D

● #15

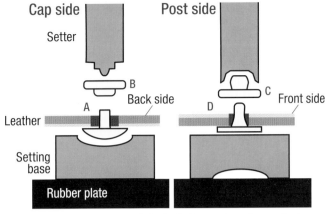

Choose the correct size of single-hole punch and snap fastener setter based on the size of snap fastener you intend to use.

Setter

Single-hole punch

Setting base (metal plate)

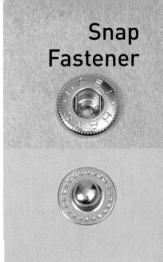

Snap Fastener

No. 5 Large

Setter Size: No. 5

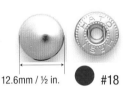

12.6mm / ½ in.   ● #18

● #10

No. 2 Small

Setter Size: No. 2

11.5mm / ⁷⁄₁₆ in.   #15

● #8

Single-hole punch size ●

Cap side

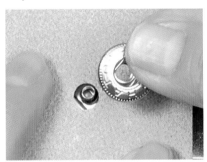

1 Place cap, size A, over the matching hole of the setting base. Place perforated leather over A. Then, place B on top.

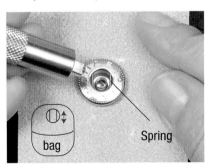

Spring

bag

2 Align the groove so as not to crush the spring and then tap lightly with a setter. Adjust so that the spring of the clasp are perpendicular to the opening of the bag (see inset diagram) and tap setter firmly.

Post side

1 Place post D, flat side down, on the setting base and cover with perforated leather.

2 Place stud C over the post and set firmly.

79

Magnet Clasp

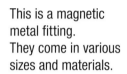

This is a magnetic metal fitting.
They come in various sizes and materials.

Depending upon the piece and the length of the tabs, it might be better to fold inward.

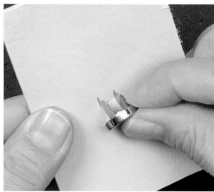

1 Press the tabs down on the grain-side to mark their positions.

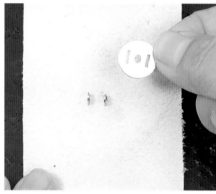

2 Make slits for the tabs to pass through. Put the tabs through and add a washer to sandwich the leather tightly.

3 Use pliers to bend the tabs. This will secure the washer to the leather.

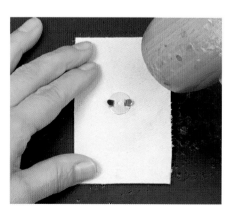

4 Strike the washer with a mallet until the tabs are bent flat.

1 Make a hole with a single-hole punch and pierce with the base.

2 From the other side, place the stud over the base and tighten the screw.

This is a metal fitting with a bulbous head. There are various sizes based on material thickness.

3 Tighten firmly with a flat-head screwdriver.

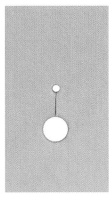

4 On the hole side of the leather (the flap, etc.) make a separate hole the size of the button head. Connect this new hole to the original with a cutter. This will make it easier to close the item.

Tuck Lock Clasp

Locks come in a variety of sizes and designs. The methods for setting them also differ. The tuck lock is one of the most commonly sold leathercrafting fittings. When attaching to thin leather, reinforce with a second piece of leather.

[Flap side] Mark positions and perforate. Insert the stud, cover with a cap, and strike with a mallet. Careful! If the tongue portion of the clasp is set too deeply into the leather it will be difficult to insert the tongue under the bar to lock in place.

[Bag side] Press the tabs into the grain-side to mark their positions. Cut with a utility knife. Pass tabs through the leather and cover with the accompanying flat washer. Bend with needlenose pliers and flatten with mallet.

There may be a difference in capacity, even if you use the same pattern as in this book, depending on the thickness, softness, and finish of the leather chosen. The metal fitting may need to be adjusted to guarantee ease of use. Attach as needed while using the two points below as a guide.

1 Attach metal fittings to the main body before sewing.
2 Fix the position of the flap side fitting after the item is complete and you have filled it. This will help verify the position.
After the item is complete and you have put things in it, fix the position of the fittings.

[Snap Fastener Position on Flap Side] Example: Glasses Case

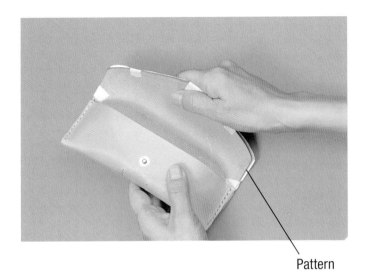

Pattern

1 Cover the flap with a paper pattern (with a centerline drawn on it) and fasten with drafting tape.

Centerline

2 Determine the hole position, etc., while confirming the position of the metal fitting on the body side. Mark for perforation.

If the flaps aren't long enough, adjust by adding leather from other parts.

Buckles and Straps

Here's how to make a cloth and leather strap, bracelets, and rings. Adjust the leather to fit your own fingers and arms. 1.8 mm / 1/16 in. thick leather

[Basic Structure of Belt or Strap]

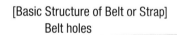

Belt holes

A

Belt loop   Buckle

B

There are basically two types of buckles.

There is a belt loop attached to A through which the belt tip can be passed. B is a stitch closure type buckle. It is not completely necessary to attach a belt loop.

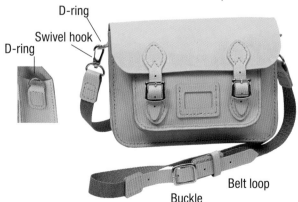

D-ring

Swivel hook

D-ring

Buckle

Belt loop

The strap can be sewn to the main body, or it can be connected with a D-ring and a swivel hook can then be used to attach to it.

Even when using a stitch closure buckle, it is best to attach a belt loop in order to prevent the belt leather itself from warping. Strap lengths vary by individual. Adjust based on the size of bag and your body structure.

How to make the strap: Make stitching holes based on the correct pattern and cut. Burnish the flesh-side and edges.

[Swivel Hook]

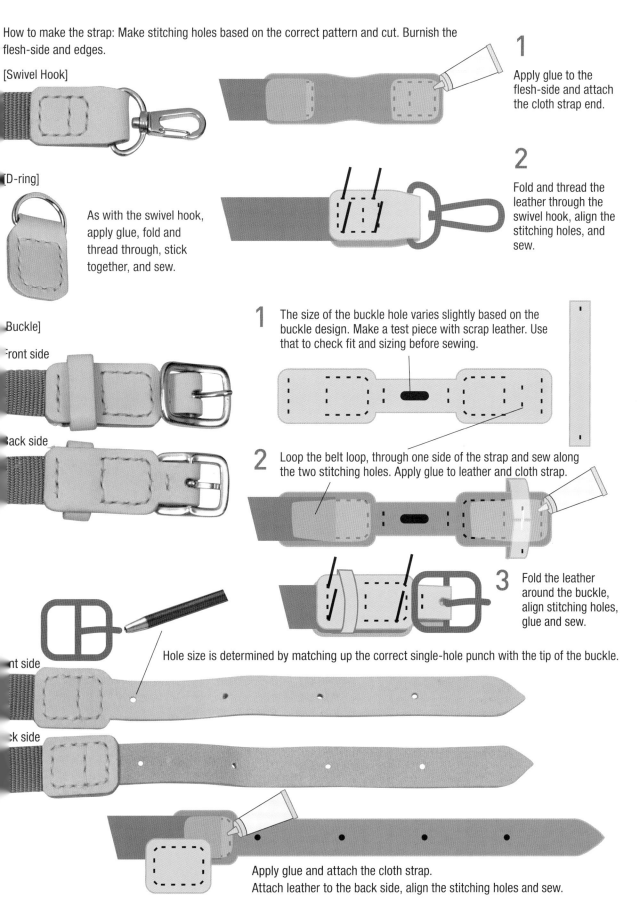

1

Apply glue to the flesh-side and attach the cloth strap end.

[D-ring]

As with the swivel hook, apply glue, fold and thread through, stick together, and sew.

2

Fold and thread the leather through the swivel hook, align the stitching holes, and sew.

[Buckle]

Front side

Back side

1 The size of the buckle hole varies slightly based on the buckle design. Make a test piece with scrap leather. Use that to check fit and sizing before sewing.

2 Loop the belt loop, through one side of the strap and sew along the two stitching holes. Apply glue to leather and cloth strap.

3 Fold the leather around the buckle, align stitching holes, glue and sew.

Hole size is determined by matching up the correct single-hole punch with the tip of the buckle.

nt side

k side

Apply glue and attach the cloth strap.
Attach leather to the back side, align the stitching holes and sew.

CHAPTER 3

Intermediate-Level Structures

These projects are a little more advanced than those in Chapter 1.

There are more parts to attach and the gussets are also attached to curved surfaces, so it looks much more complicated. In reality, if you do everything in order and follow the guidelines it's not as difficult as it appears. The key here is to sew the gussets neatly.

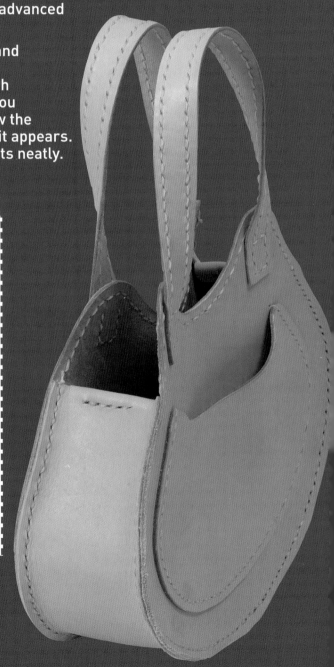

Refer to Chapter 4, "Leathercrafting Basics," to assemble.

Chapter 3 "HOW TO" explains the production steps.

★ Be sure to double check the number of stitching holes and their positions on the patterns.

★ The gluing methods and start positions for sewing are simplified because the figures in the "HOW TO:" sections are small. So, be sure to follow the procedures laid out in Chapter 4.

★ The finishing process is omitted. See p. 136.

The most important part of curved gussets is the gluing, found on p. 126 of Chapter 4 and called "Gluing Leather." Refer to that section while gluing.

1 Moisten the seam allowance.

2 Bend the seam allowance.

3 Glue the gusset and sew.

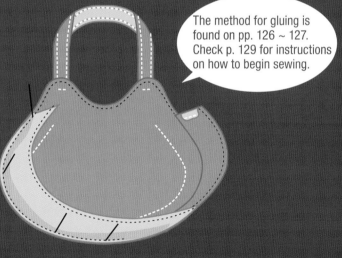

The method for gluing is found on pp. 126 ~ 127. Check p. 129 for instructions on how to begin sewing.

Check the number of stitching holes and any other mark on the pattern.

★ Although these steps are not shown to make the diagrams easier to understand, remember to apply them: "temporarily stabilize key areas with thread," and "glue while sandwiching a piece of paper between the leather pieces and aligning the stitching holes section by section."

★ If the gusset is a separate part altogether, it can look a little dented when attached to the bag. To fix this lightly moisten the entire bag, stuff with an old towel, shape, and then dry. This will produce a cleanly shaped bulge.

pattern

Oval-shaped side gusset

Binoculars Case

Leather thickness = 1.8 mm / ¹/₁₆ in.
Oil-tanned leather

Although sized to accommodate various binoculars, it is recommended to decide upon the position of the Sam Browne stud after sewing. This will allow for fine adjustments.

HOW TO:

1 Punch stitching holes and cut the leather according to the pattern. Burnish the flesh-side and edges.

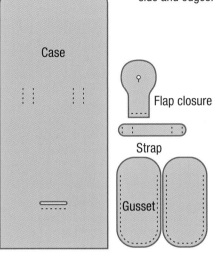

Case

Flap closure

Strap

Gusset

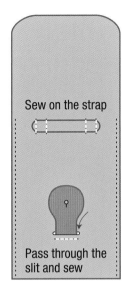

Sew on the strap

Pass through the slit and sew

2 Glue the end of the flap closure and the strap to the main body.

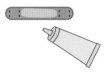

Glue

3 Moisten the seam allowance of the gusset and then fold towards the grain-side.

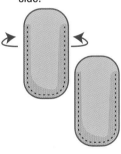

4 While referencing the pattern, align the gusset and the case with the stitching holes. Then, glue and stitch.

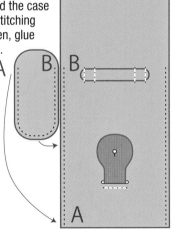

A B B

A

A

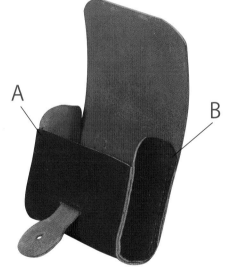

A

B

5 After inserting the binoculars, fold the flap closure over the flap to determine the Sam Browne stud position. Mark by denting the leather. Remove the flap closure and perforate in the center of the dents. Add the Sam Browne stud. See p. 81.

6 Tie a thin string of leather to the strap. If the string doesn't go through the openings easily, moisten and widen the openings with a punch or screwdriver.

Before aging process has been applied

Bottom-Gusset Clutch Bag

pattern

Leather thickness = 1.8 mm / 1/16 in.   AGED

The image is that of a paper lunch bag. A belt is added to hold the flap down.

Bag bottom

90

HOW TO:

1 Punch stitching holes and cut the leather according to the pattern. Burnish the flesh-side and edges. Mark the ○ position on the flesh-side.

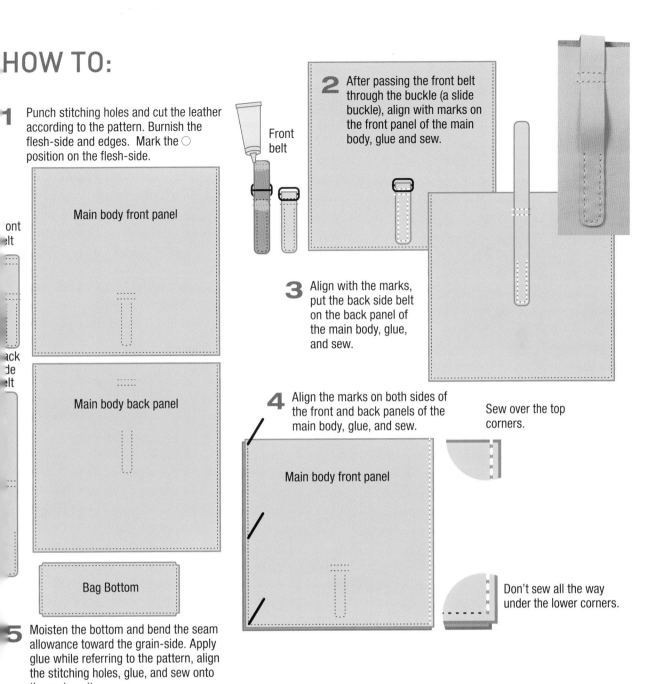

Front belt

Main body front panel

ont
:lt

ick
le
:lt

Main body back panel

Bag Bottom

2 After passing the front belt through the buckle (a slide buckle), align with marks on the front panel of the main body, glue and sew.

Front belt

3 Align with the marks, put the back side belt on the back panel of the main body, glue, and sew.

4 Align the marks on both sides of the front and back panels of the main body, glue, and sew.

Main body front panel

Sew over the top corners.

Don't sew all the way under the lower corners.

5 Moisten the bottom and bend the seam allowance toward the grain-side. Apply glue while referring to the pattern, align the stitching holes, glue, and sew onto the main unit.

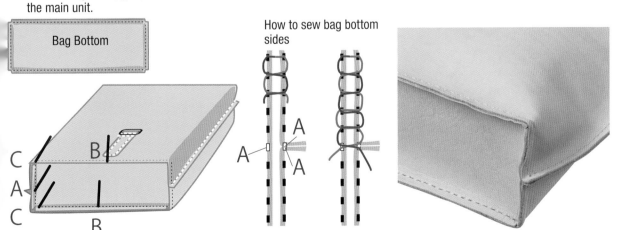

Bag Bottom

C
B
A
C
B

How to sew bag bottom sides

A
A
A
A

pattern

Odd-shaped bag bottom

Bicolor Tote Bag

Leather thickness = 1.8 mm / 1/16 in.
Tanned leather and oil-tanned leather

Enjoy re-creating a canvas tote bag with leather.

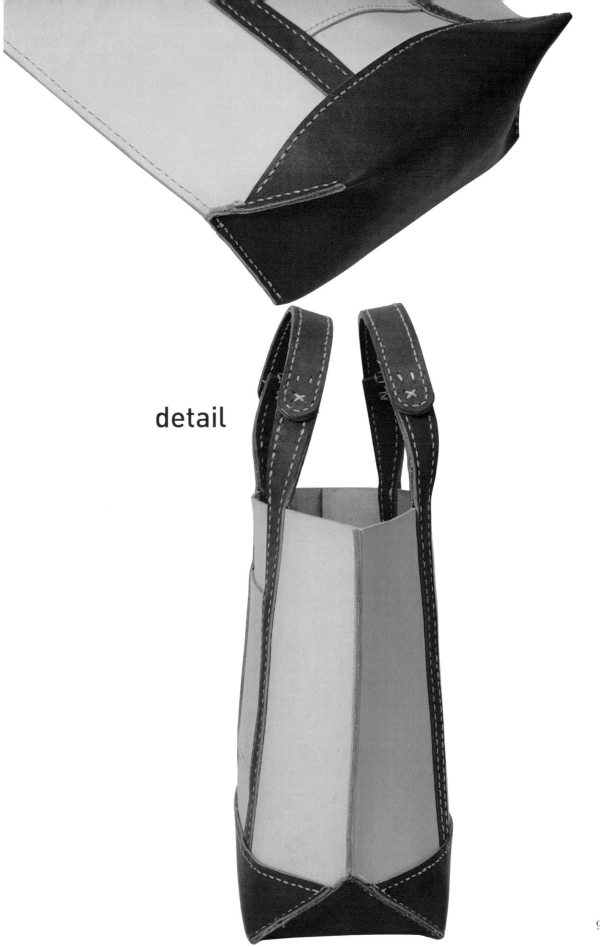

detail

93

HOW TO:

1 Punch stitching holes and cut the leather according to the pattern. Burnish the flesh-side and edges. Mark ○ positions on the flesh-side.

2 Apply glue to seam allowance of pocket. Align stitching holes while referencing pattern and attach pocket to the front of main unit. Sew between areas marked B.

3 Attach handle to main body.
Align stitching holes of front and back of handle, while referencing the pattern. Glue a few holes below G while sandwiching the bag body between the handles.

Glue the handle to the main body while aligning the stitching holes.

Place handle pieces above the pocket.

4 Sew the back and front of the handles, as well as the pocket and main body, together.

End here

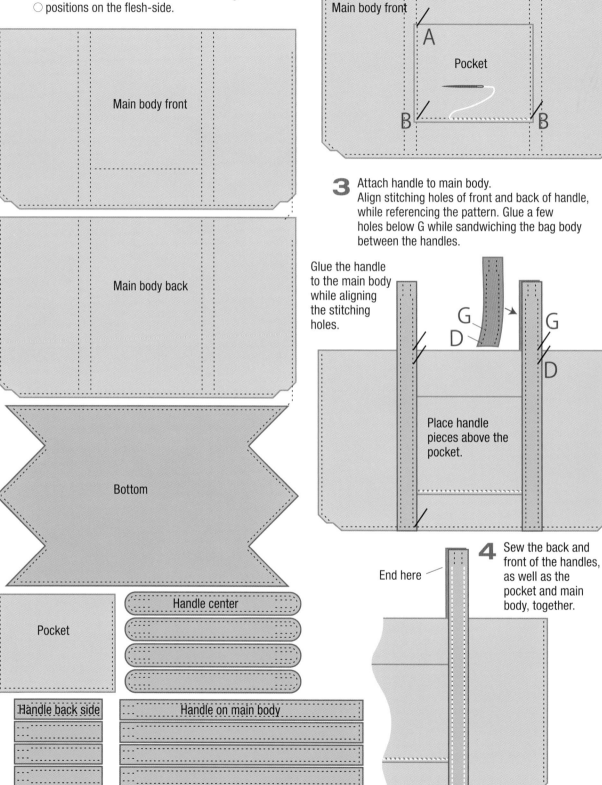

Main body front

Main body back

Bottom

Pocket

Handle center

Handle back side

Handle on main body

Main body front

A

Pocket

B   B

G
D   G
D

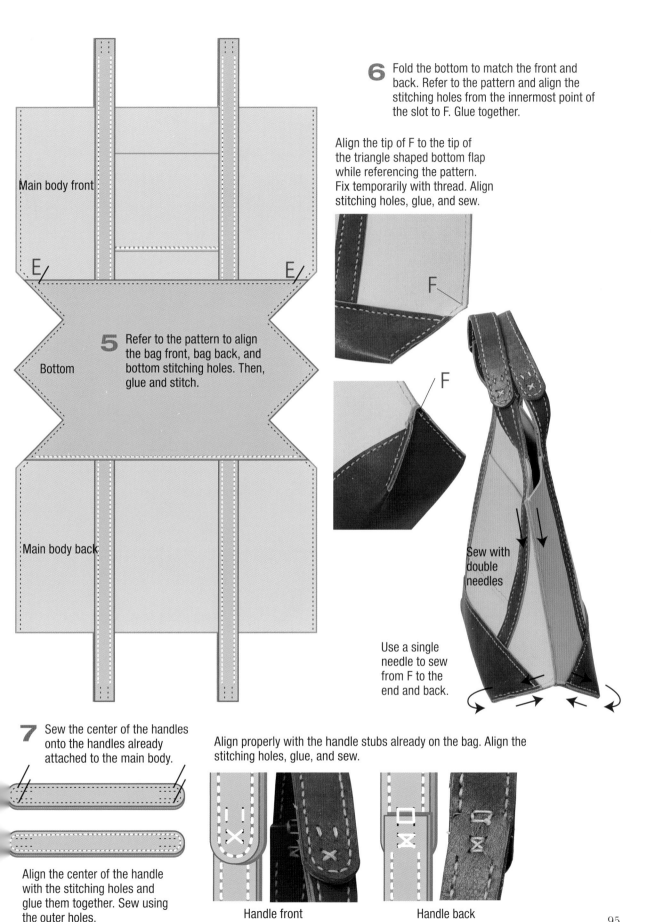

Main body front

E

5 Refer to the pattern to align the bag front, bag back, and bottom stitching holes. Then, glue and stitch.

Bottom

E

Main body back

6 Fold the bottom to match the front and back. Refer to the pattern and align the stitching holes from the innermost point of the slot to F. Glue together.

Align the tip of F to the tip of the triangle shaped bottom flap while referencing the pattern. Fix temporarily with thread. Align stitching holes, glue, and sew.

F

F

Sew with double needles

Use a single needle to sew from F to the end and back.

7 Sew the center of the handles onto the handles already attached to the main body.

Align the center of the handle with the stitching holes and glue them together. Sew using the outer holes.

Align properly with the handle stubs already on the bag. Align the stitching holes, glue, and sew.

Handle front

Handle back

95

pattern

Three separate pieces

Round-Bottom Shoulder Bag

Leather thickness = 1.8 mm / ¹/₁₆ in. **AGED**

This is a beautiful bag with an appliqué decorated flap. The decoration also serves to hide the back of the snap. The strap is the same adjustable cloth and leather one seen previously. Refer to p. 84.

detail

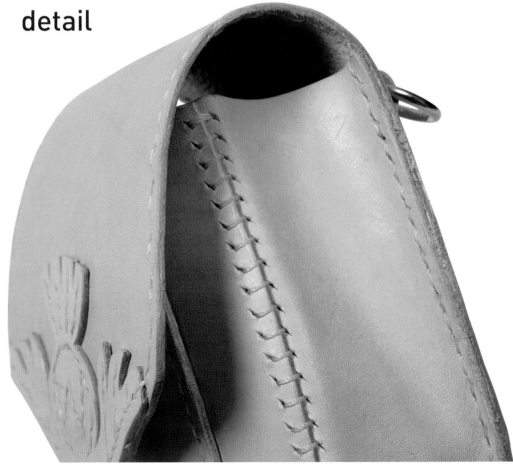

HOW TO:

1 Punch stitching holes and cut the leather according to the pattern. Burnish the flesh-side and edges. Mark positions of ○ on the flesh-side.

Leather piece for D-ring

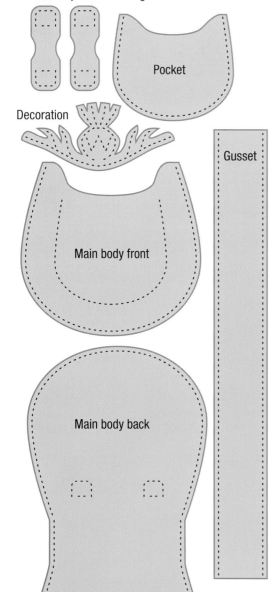

Decoration

Pocket

Gusset

Main body front

Main body back

2 Attach magnetic clasp pieces to both the pocket and flap on the main body. See p. 80.

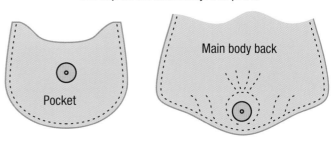

Main body back

Pocket

3 Apply glue to seam allowance on the pocket. Align stitching holes on front of main body, while referencing the pattern, glue, and sew.

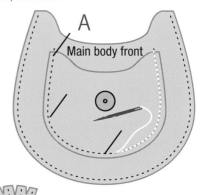

A

Main body front

4 Sew only the part shown in the figure.

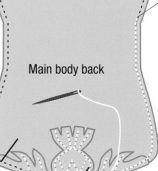

Glue to the back of the main body and sew.

E

Main body back

5 Match up the marks and glue the decoration on the flap. Glue, and sew. Sew around to B.

6 Attach D-rings to the back of the main body.

Pass the leather through the D-ring, bend it back on itself, and glue. See p. 84.

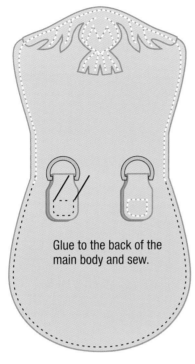

Glue to the back of the main body and sew.

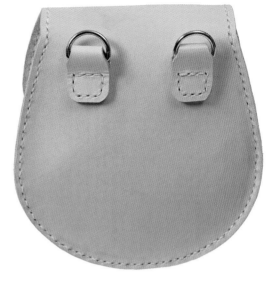

7 Moisten the seam allowance of the gusset and fold.

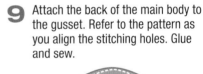

Fold the front side of the main body toward the flesh-side.

Fold the back side of the main body toward the grain-side.

8 Cover the front of the main body with the gusset and glue while aligning the stitching holes. Reference the pattern. See "Butt Stitch" on p. 75.

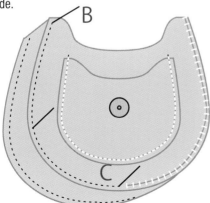

B

C

9 Attach the back of the main body to the gusset. Refer to the pattern as you align the stitching holes. Glue and sew.

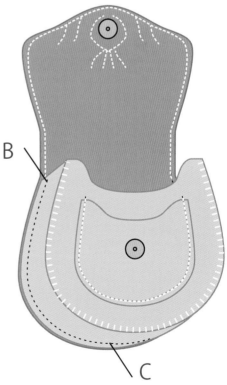

B

C

★ The bag straps in this book are all constructed the same way.
Refer to p. 84, "Buckles and Straps."

Gusset

pattern

Three separate pieces

Small Bag with Handles

Leather thickness = 1.8 mm / 1/16 in.   AGED

This is such a cute little bag. The stitching really accentuates the overall style.

100

HOW TO:

1 Punch stitching holes and cut the leather according to the pattern. Burnish the flesh-side and edges. Mark ○ positions on the flesh-side.

Gusset

Main body front

Main body back

Pocket

Handle

3 Sew the handle according to the figure.

Stop stitching

Stop stitching

4 Apply glue to both ends of the handle. Align stitching holes on both the back and front of the main body. Sew.

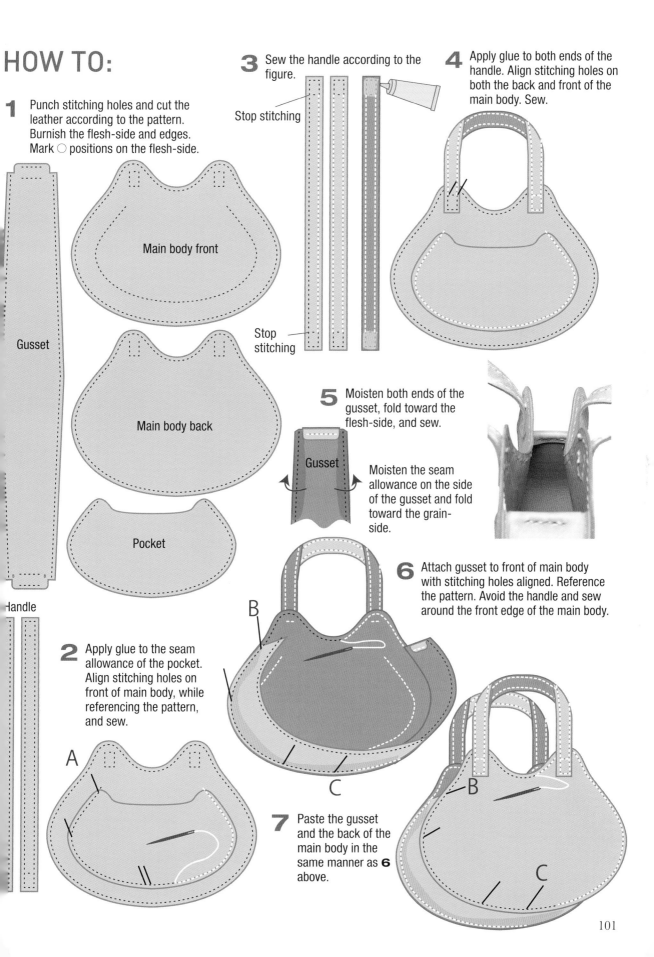

5 Moisten both ends of the gusset, fold toward the flesh-side, and sew.

Gusset

Moisten the seam allowance on the side of the gusset and fold toward the grain-side.

6 Attach gusset to front of main body with stitching holes aligned. Reference the pattern. Avoid the handle and sew around the front edge of the main body.

B

C

2 Apply glue to the seam allowance of the pocket. Align stitching holes on front of main body, while referencing the pattern, and sew.

A

7 Paste the gusset and the back of the main body in the same manner as **6** above.

B

C

pattern

Round Bag

Leather thickness = 1.8 mm / 1/16 in. Oil-tanned leather

A gusset with a zipper is sewn on a perfect circle. This lovely little piece is accented with small pockets.

Gusset and two separate body pieces

HOW TO:

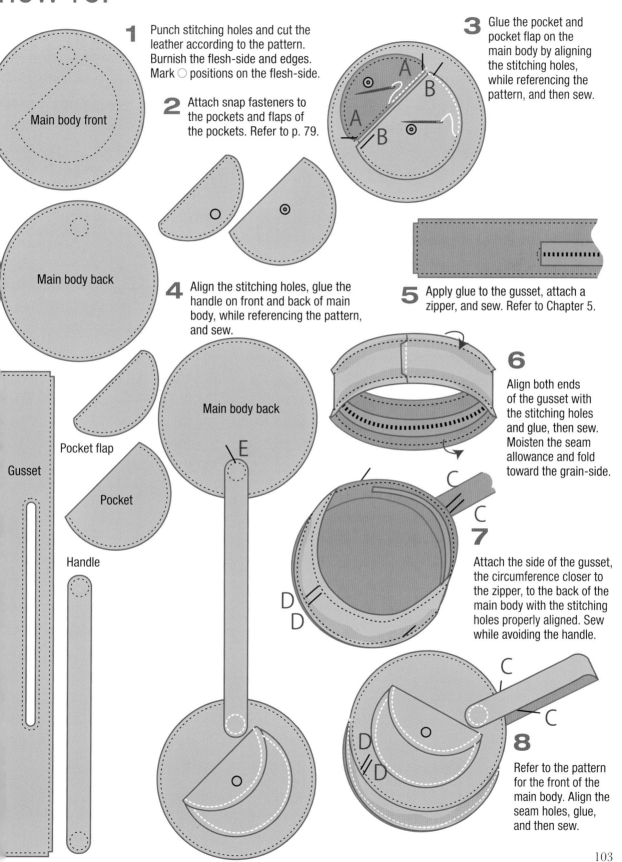

1 Punch stitching holes and cut the leather according to the pattern. Burnish the flesh-side and edges. Mark ○ positions on the flesh-side.

2 Attach snap fasteners to the pockets and flaps of the pockets. Refer to p. 79.

3 Glue the pocket and pocket flap on the main body by aligning the stitching holes, while referencing the pattern, and then sew.

4 Align the stitching holes, glue the handle on front and back of main body, while referencing the pattern, and sew.

5 Apply glue to the gusset, attach a zipper, and sew. Refer to Chapter 5.

6 Align both ends of the gusset with the stitching holes and glue, then sew. Moisten the seam allowance and fold toward the grain-side.

7 Attach the side of the gusset, the circumference closer to the zipper, to the back of the main body with the stitching holes properly aligned. Sew while avoiding the handle.

8 Refer to the pattern for the front of the main body. Align the seam holes, glue, and then sew.

Main body front

Main body back

Main body back

Gusset

Pocket flap

Pocket

Handle

103

pattern

Four-sided gusset

Square Bag

Leather thickness = 1.8 mm / $\frac{1}{16}$ in.　AGED

The gusset is made by attaching four parts together. It looks difficult, but if you follow the symbols on the pattern and match the gusset and main body together well, you'll construct a strong, well-proportioned bag.

detail

HOW TO:

1 Punch stitching holes and cut the leather according to the pattern. Burnish the flesh-side and edges. Mark positions of ○ on the flesh-side.

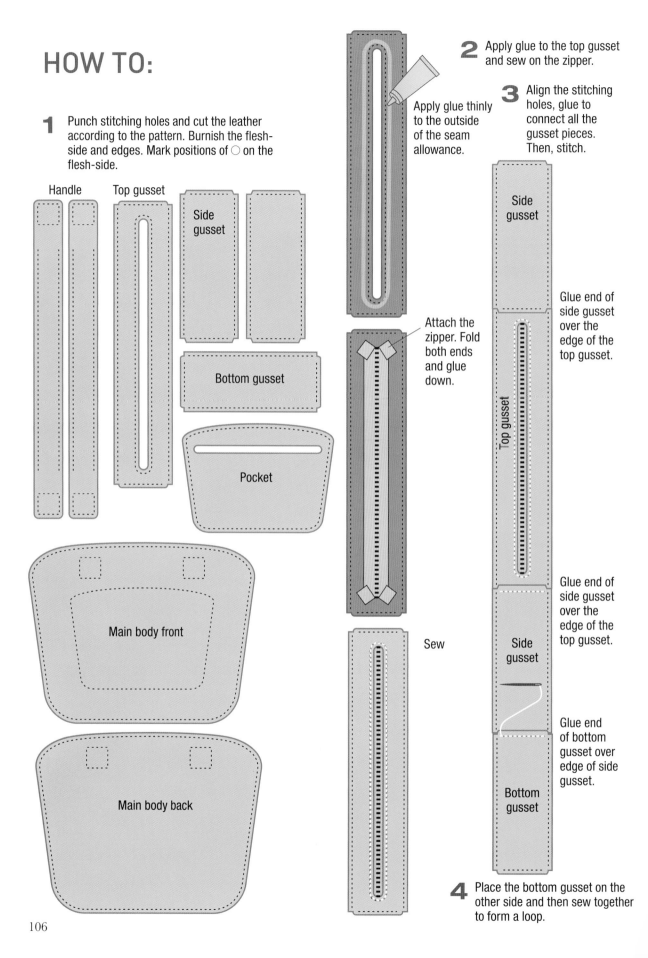

Handle

Top gusset

Side gusset

Bottom gusset

Pocket

Main body front

Main body back

2 Apply glue to the top gusset and sew on the zipper.

Apply glue thinly to the outside of the seam allowance.

3 Align the stitching holes, glue to connect all the gusset pieces. Then, stitch.

Attach the zipper. Fold both ends and glue down.

Side gusset

Top gusset

Glue end of side gusset over the edge of the top gusset.

Glue end of side gusset over the edge of the top gusset.

Side gusset

Sew

Glue end of bottom gusset over edge of side gusset.

Bottom gusset

4 Place the bottom gusset on the other side and then sew together to form a loop.

5 Fold the center of the handle in half. Apply glue to the seam allowance, align stitching holes, and sew.

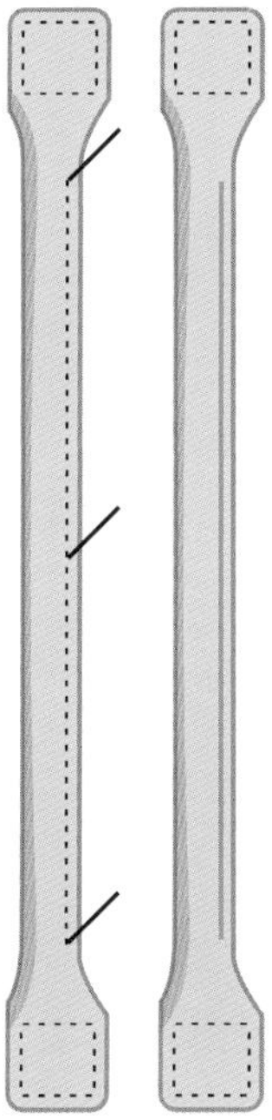

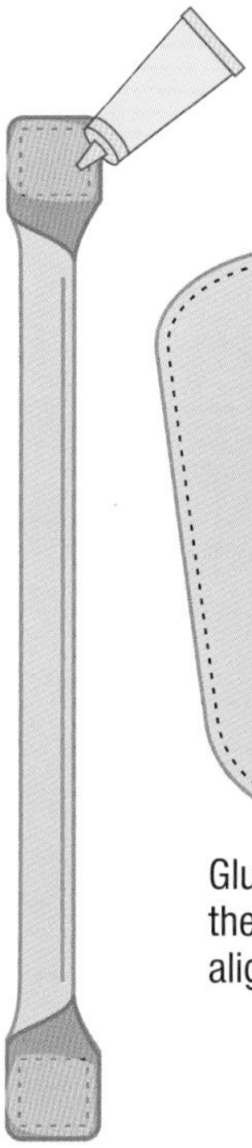

6 Glue both ends of the handle on the front of the main body, align stitching holes, and sew.

Attach the handle to the back of the main body as well.

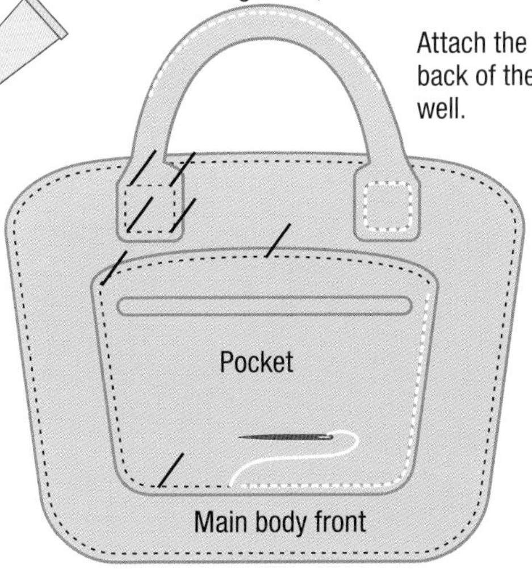

Pocket

Main body front

Glue is applied to the seam allowance of the pocket and then the stitching holes are aligned and sewn.

7 Moisten the seam allowance of the gusset and fold it toward the grain-side.

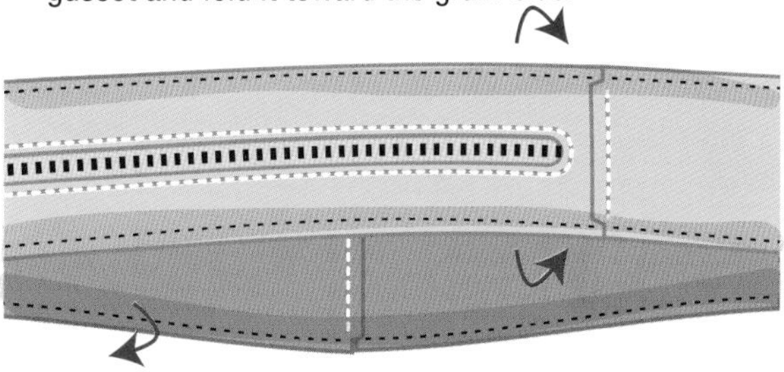

8 Attach gusset to the main body.

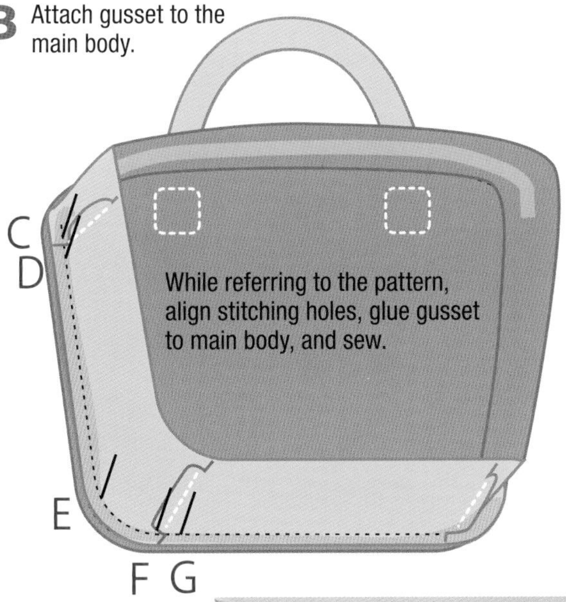

C
D

While referring to the pattern, align stitching holes, glue gusset to main body, and sew.

E

F G

Attach the other side in the same manner.

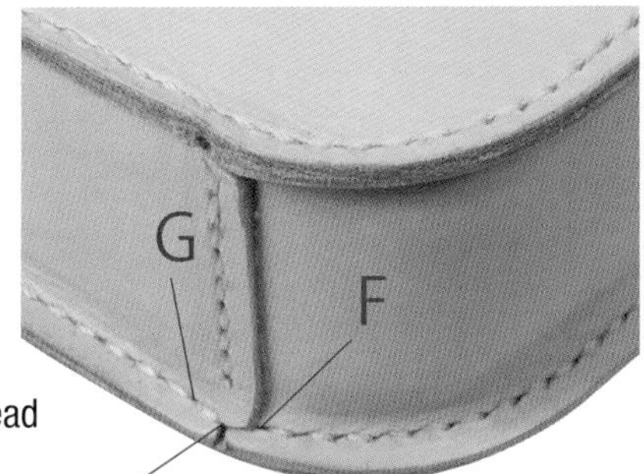

G

F

Pass the first thread through the gap between the overlapped gussets.

pattern

Three-sided gusset

Satchel-Style Bag

Leather thickness = 1.8 mm / $1/16$ in.

It's a little small, but you can probably tell this is a British student–style bag. The strap is the same as in other designs. Refer to p. 84.

detail

HOW TO:

1 Punch stitching holes and cut the leather according to the pattern. Burnish the flesh-side and edges. Mark positions of ○ on the flesh-side.

2 Attach the necessary parts to the pocket. For the frame of the pocket be sure to properly align the marks, glue the seam allowance, and sew. The belt buckle piece is passed through the buckle, bent back on itself, glued, and then sewn to the pocket. Refer to p. 84

Bend back on itself. Match these holes.

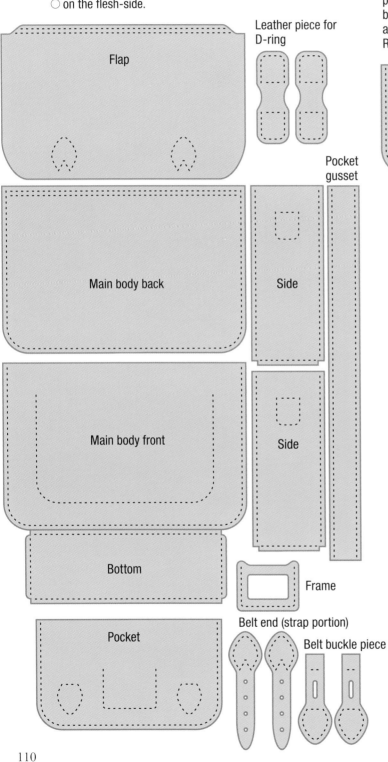

Leather piece for D-ring

Pocket gusset

Flap

Main body back

Side

Main body front

Side

Bottom

Pocket

Frame

Belt end (strap portion)

Belt buckle piece

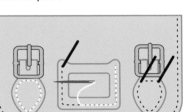
Align stitching holes.

3 Putting the gusset on your pocket. Molsten the gusset and bend the seam allowance toward the grain-side. Apply glue, align stitching holes based on the pattern, and sew. See p. 127.

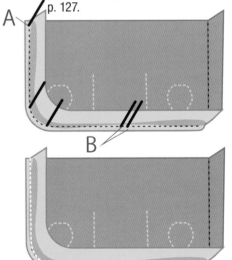
A

B

4 Attach D-ring leather to side of main body.

Glue to the side of the body and sew.

Pass leather through D-ring, bend back on itself, and glue. See p. 84.

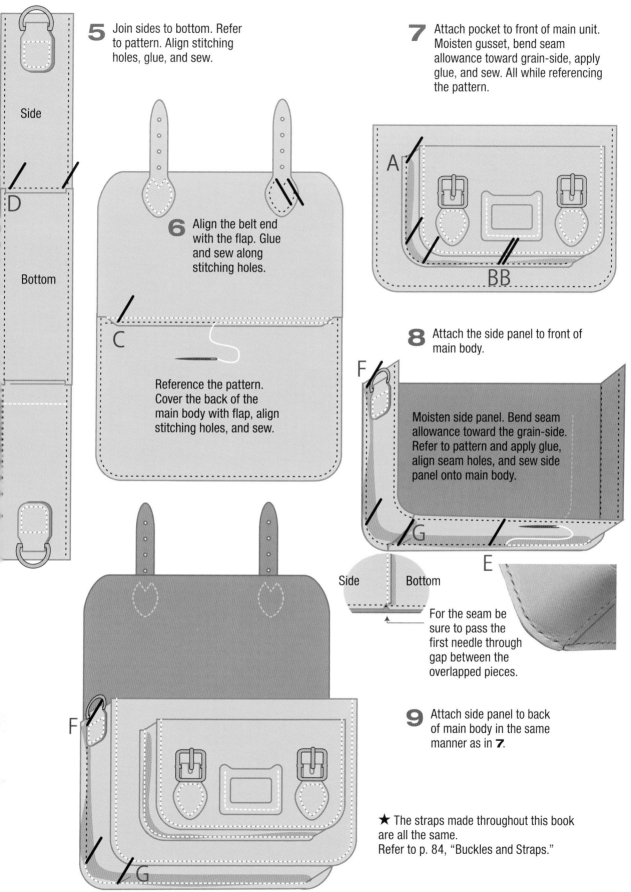

5 Join sides to bottom. Refer to pattern. Align stitching holes, glue, and sew.

Side

D

Bottom

6 Align the belt end with the flap. Glue and sew along stitching holes.

C

Reference the pattern. Cover the back of the main body with flap, align stitching holes, and sew.

7 Attach pocket to front of main unit. Moisten gusset, bend seam allowance toward grain-side, apply glue, and sew. All while referencing the pattern.

A

BB

8 Attach the side panel to front of main body.

F

Moisten side panel. Bend seam allowance toward the grain-side. Refer to pattern and apply glue, align seam holes, and sew side panel onto main body.

G

E

Side   Bottom

For the seam be sure to pass the first needle through gap between the overlapped pieces.

9 Attach side panel to back of main body in the same manner as in **7**.

F

G

★ The straps made throughout this book are all the same.
Refer to p. 84, "Buckles and Straps."

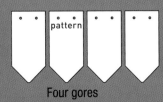

Four gores

Drawstring Bag

Leather = Calf

A drawstring-style bag made from soft calf leather. Sew, then turn right-side out for a lovely finish.
This is a very easy to fashion bag with four gores.

HOW TO:

1 Punch stitching holes and cut the leather according to the pattern. Burnish the edges of the bag opening. Mark ○ positions on the flesh-side.

2 Face grain-sides toward each other, align the stitching holes, glue, and finally stitch.

Make notches in the corner seam allowances so that the piece can be easily turned right-side out.

3 Turn right-side out.

4 Thread the thin leather straps.

5 Attach tassel to the straps.

Align and paste to the strap tips.

Glue this portion of the tassel.

Punch a hole using a lacing needle.

Wrap around the thin leather strap.

6 mm / ¼ in.

End stitch

Strap

Bag

Tassel

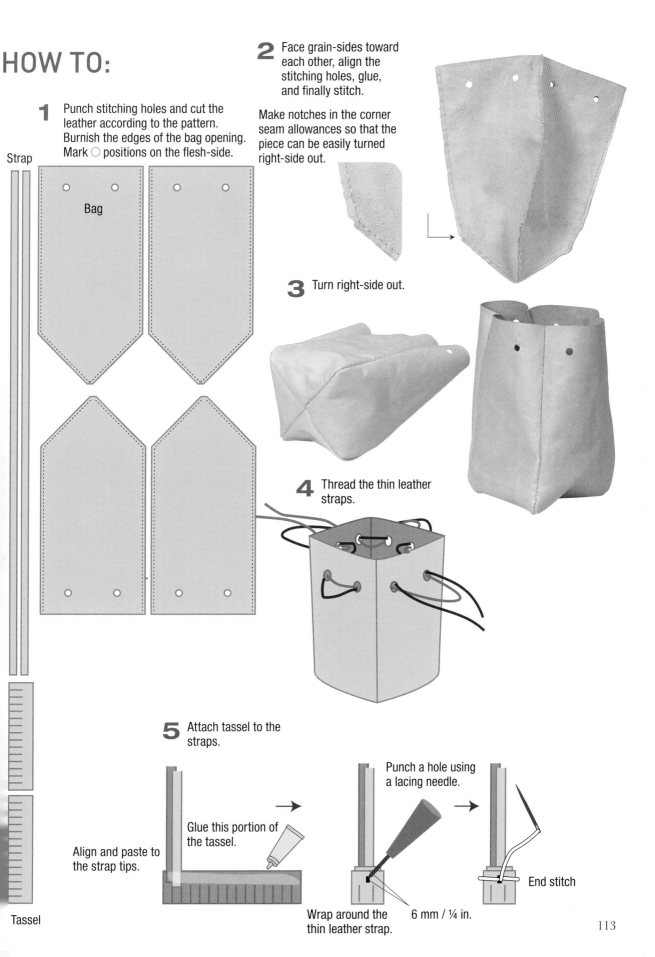

113

CHAPTER 4

Leathercrafting Basics

Learn the how-tos that are absolutely necessary for making any design. We'll use the Basic Pen Case to, step by step, teach you each essential skill. All projects in the previous chapters use the basic concepts here.

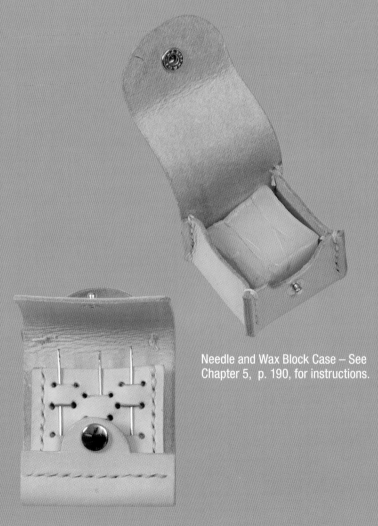

Needle and Wax Block Case — See Chapter 5, p. 190, for instructions.

pattern

Making a Basic Pen Case

A simple pen case that can be closed with a strap. We will use the most basic leathercrafting processes for this project.

Preparing the Patterns

Photocopy the patterns you will need.
Make photocopies of the actual sized
patterns for each item required.

125%

Enlargement ratio of the pattern

Enlarge the paper pattern to 125%.

[Basic Pen Case Pattern]

Dimensions are displayed
for long strings, etc.

Pattern outline (includes seam allowance)
Cut leather along this line.

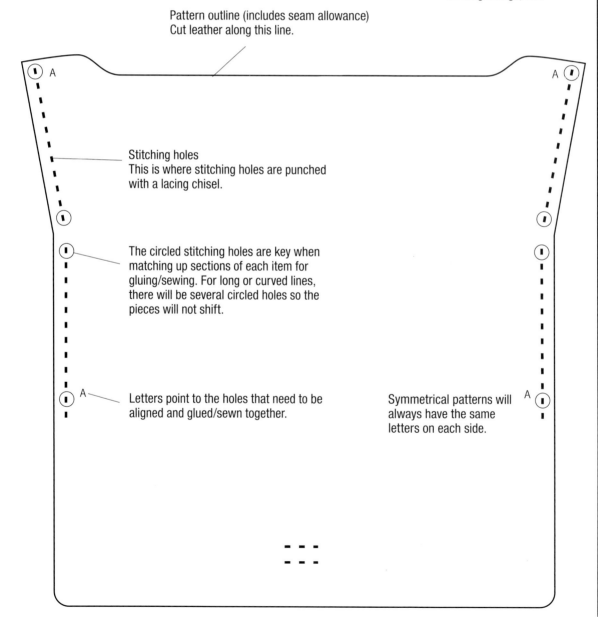

Stitching holes
This is where stitching holes are punched
with a lacing chisel.

The circled stitching holes are key when
matching up sections of each item for
gluing/sewing. For long or curved lines,
there will be several circled holes so the
pieces will not shift.

Letters point to the holes that need to be
aligned and glued/sewn together.

Symmetrical patterns will
always have the same
letters on each side.

1 To prevent distortion, be sure to make your pattern photocopies while firmly opening the pages.

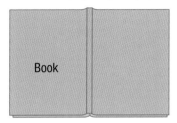

Book

Open the book spine firmly

Make your photocopy according to the enlargement ratio specified on the page.
When making photocopies at a copy center, bring a ruler with you and make certain of the photocopied gauge length.

2 Roughly cut out the photocopy.

3 Glue on a sheet of simili paper or thick copy paper. Use a glue stick. Glue the seam allowance area of the pattern firmly to prevent it from falling off.

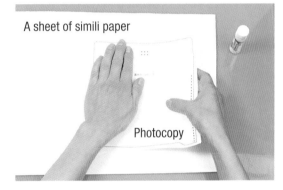

A sheet of simili paper

Photocopy

4 Make sure the dimensions are correct – and that the right angles and horizontal lines are not misaligned – and then cut along the contour lines.

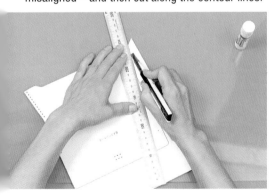

5 For the long leather piece, the outline is copied onto the leather while measuring its dimensions with a ruler. So, you only need to cut out the marked part.

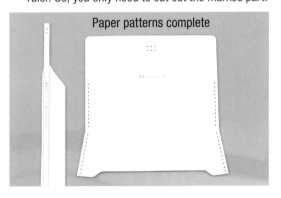

Paper patterns complete

★ If you want to carry something like a mobile phone or binoculars you may need to modify the patterns used in this book. Check the size of the item by marking out the copied patterns in advance. Chapter 5 contains methods for modifying pattern sizes.

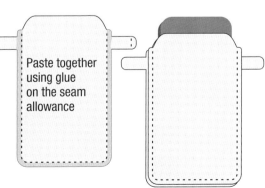

Paste together using glue on the seam allowance

Make sure it is large enough to hold the desired item. The thicker the leather, the more leeway you must allow. It's easy to check the sizing by wrapping the desired piece of leather around your chosen item.

Rough Cutting

Roughly cut large pieces of leather to make them easier to work with.

If the leather is warped, moisten the grain-side and the flesh-side with a wet sponge and adjust to make it flat. After the leather has completely dried, tape the patterns on.

 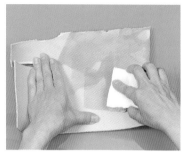 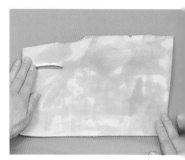

[Arrangement] Place the required number of patterns on the leather.

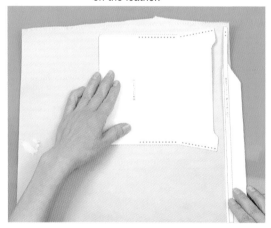

★ For long parts, such as straps, cut the leather as large as possible without going overboard. Refer to p. 123 and cut the strap before rough cutting the main body.

1 Place the pattern for each item on the grain-side of the leather, and then secure in several places with drafting tape. At the edge of the leather, secure the pattern by taping to the flesh-side.

2 Place a vinyl cutting board underneath and cut out the leather roughly with a utility knife.
Make sure to press down on the surface of the leather, not the pattern, when cutting the leather as the pattern will move eas
(Refer to precautions listed on p. 122 when using a utility knif

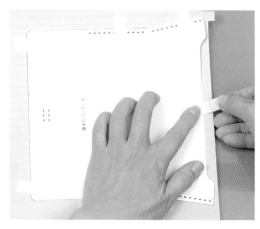

Rough-cut leather

Transfer the pattern outline onto the grain-side of the leather using a scratch awl.

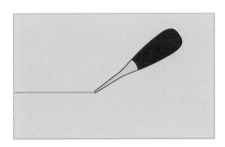

In order to prevent damage to the leather, place the tip of the scratch awl at an angle to score the line. Do not use the point of the scratch awl.

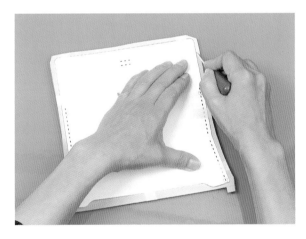

1

For straight lines, align a ruler with the edge of the pattern and then score.
Do not cross over top of the drafting tape as the scratch awl tip will tear the tape.
After punching the stitching holes, and after peeling off the tape, connect the scored lines.
For curved lines, hold the pattern and then score a precise line by following alongside the pattern with the scratch awl tip.

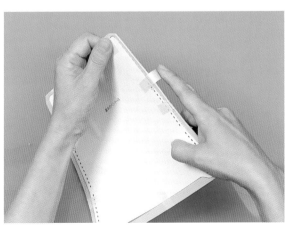

2

If the pattern is moving too easily, wrap the drafting tape around to the flesh-side to help secure it.

Punching Stitching Holes

Use a 5 mm wide, four prong lacing chisel to punch the stitching holes marked on the pattern.

The number of stitching holes is made to match each seam where they join. So, be very careful not to accidentally change the number of stitching holes.

A little practice is needed to be able to punch a neat hole straight down through to the back.

For beginners, it's best to practice punching holes in a piece of scrap leather.

[Hole Punching Basics]

Place leather on a rubber plate so that the direction of the stitching holes is perpendicular to you.

Place lacing chisel perpendicular to leather and then strike with a wooden mallet a couple of times to punch holes.

Make sure that holes are punched all the way through.

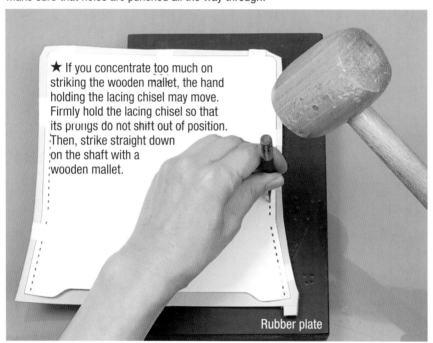

★ If you concentrate too much on striking the wooden mallet, the hand holding the lacing chisel may move. Firmly hold the lacing chisel so that its prongs do not shift out of position. Then, strike straight down on the shaft with a wooden mallet.

Rubber plate

Attention!!

When the direction of the stitching holes is horizontal to you, the lacing chisel tends to slant.

The holding power of drafting tape is actually fairly weak, so be sure the pattern doesn't shift out of position.

Tools for punching holes, such as lacing chisels, are very sharp-edged. Work with caution.

[Straight Stitching Holes]

1 Use a four-prong lacing chisel. Place the prongs of the lacing chisel on the hole positions of the pattern.

2 Place the lacing chisel perpendicular to the leather.

Hold the bottom part of the lacing chisel and make sure your hand touches the leather – this will stabilize the chisel and, as a result, the prongs will stay in position.

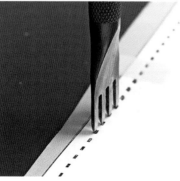

[Curved-Line Stitching Holes]

Use a two-prong lacing chisel.
Place the prong on the curve and punch holes in the same manner as the four-prong lacing chisel.

[Single Stitching Hole]

Pierce firmly with a lacing needle.

[Round Holes and Markings for Metal Fittings]

Mark center of hole with a scratch awl.
See p. 76 for punching grommet holes.

[Marking]

After punching all the holes, pierce the circled stitch holes with a scratch awl. Then, turn the leather over and mark the pierced position with a pencil from the flesh-side.
Do not use markers! They'll mark the edges and grain-side of the leather.

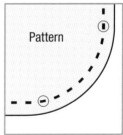

Pattern

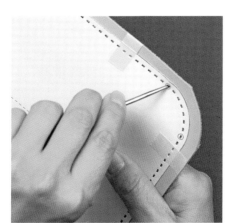 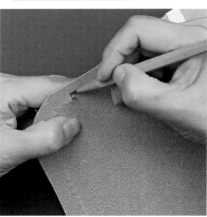

Cutting

Put the leather on a vinyl board and then cut with a large-sized utility knife.

Compared to materials of similar thickness, leather is easier to cut. However, it can be stretched and warped easily so you must be careful to cut along the scored scratch awl line.

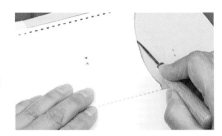

[Peel Off the Pattern]

For the taped areas, connect the outline marked in the previous step as you peel each piece of tape off.

[Cutting Leather]

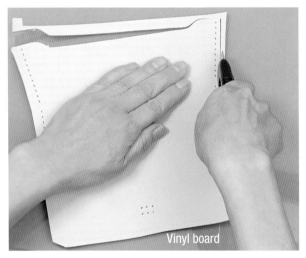

Vinyl board

Place the vinyl board on a working surface and put the leather on top. Be sure that it is perpendicular to your body. Firmly press down on the leather and then slowly and carefully cut the leather along the scored line with a large utility knife.

Do not cut the leather if the pattern is still taped as patterns taped on leather tend to come off very easily.

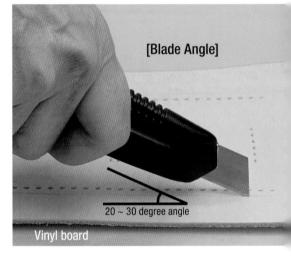

[Blade Angle]

20 ~ 30 degree angle

Vinyl board

Cut the leather by holding the utility knife so the blade is angled at 20 ~ 30 degrees to the leather.
If the blade angles to the left or right, the cut edge will be slanted.
Pay special attention when you cut thick leather.
Be sure to snap off the blade often so you are always cut with a fresh razor.

[Precautions When Cutting Leather]

Do not use a ruler as a guideline as the leather is fairly slippery.

Keep your fingers away from the utility knife blade.

If you cut the leather horizontally, the cut line often won't be straight.

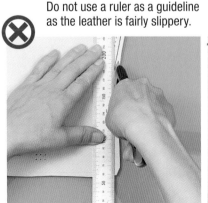

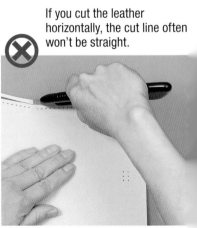

[Cutting the Strap]

1 Use a ruler to score a line with a scratch awl according to the dimensions on the pattern.

2 Remove the ruler and cut along the marks. Start from the outer edge of the leather.

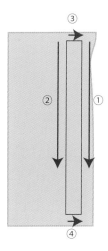

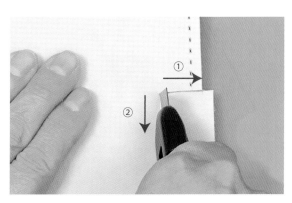

[Cutting Corners]

1 Firmly place the blade at the corner and then proceed to cut toward the exterior.
2 Once again place the blade at the corner and then cut steadily along the remaining line.

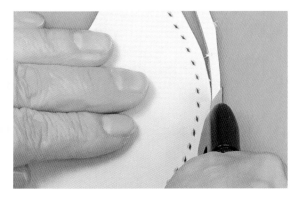

[Cutting Curves]

Always keep the direction of the cut perpendicular to your body by rotating the leather and cutting little by little.

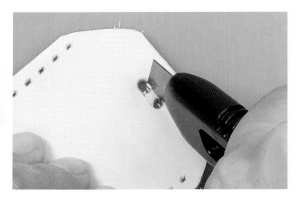

[Cutting Elongated Holes with Rounded Corners]

Start by punching a hole at the perforation mark.

Elongated holes with rounded corners can be cut cleanly by first punching holes at both ends. Then connect them with a utility knife.

Cut with a utility knife to connect the holes.

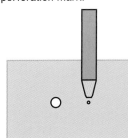

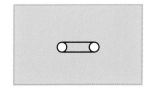

Burnishing the Flesh-Side

Smooth out the coarse flesh-side surface.

On the flesh-side of the leather, the fibers become grainy and come off as the leather breaks in. In order to prevent this, burnish the flesh-side by applying Tokonole (Tragacanth substitute).
Do not burnish gluing areas as burnished surfaces hinder the adhesive action of glue.

Do not apply Tokonole

1

Put some Tokonole on a piece of cloth, and spread it lightly onto the flesh-side of the leather. If Tokonole is spread all the way to the edge, it may cross over to the grain-side of the leather. This will result in marring of the grain-side, so pay attention when you apply Tokonole near leather edges. If Tokonole spreads onto the stitching holes, it should not cause a problem. However, it does hinder the adhesive action of the glue, so try to avoid it.

2

Once the Tokonole has pretty much dried (i.e., it doesn't feel tacky), burnish the flesh-side by sliding a slicker back and forth over the leather. Doing this will smooth the fibers of the flesh-side, which then becomes lustrous.

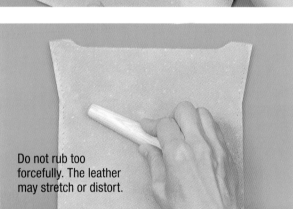

Do not rub too forcefully. The leather may stretch or distort.

Use the tip of a utility knife to scrape off the Tokonole where glue is applied.

Before burnishing

After burnishing

Burnish the edge of the leather by applying Tokonole.
Similar to burnishing the flesh-side, leather fibers on the edge will become smooth and lustrous.
Burnish the edges of the seams after stitching.
Burnish handles, pockets, and fastening parts before attaching to the main body.

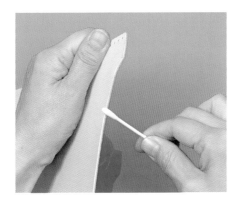

1

Put a small amount of Tokonole on a cotton swab and then spread it along the edge, while being careful not to touch the grain-side of the leather.

Burnish after stitching is complete.

Coil narrow straps or cords to make application easy.

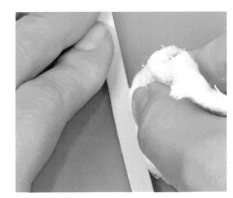

2

After the leather has nearly dried, begin to burnish the edge.
For burnishing leather that is approximately 2 mm ($1/16$ in.) thick, place on a table, then put a piece of cloth over the edge and rub both sides.

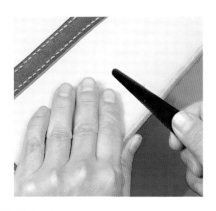

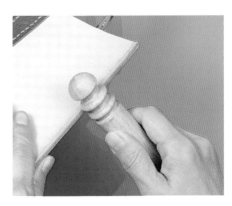

3

Use a dresser to work with seam edges.
Apply Tokonole. After it has nearly dried, burnish the edge with the slicker.

Before burnishing

After burnishing

Gluing Leather

Glue the seam allowances together while aligning the stitching holes.

This book uses glue that needs to be applied to both pieces you intend to bond together.
Apply glue to both sides and allow to dry. Then, bond by applying pressure.

Before bonding, make sure that the number of stitching holes matches.

[Gluing While Matching Stitching Holes]

1 Apply glue to the seam allowance and spread outward with a spatula.
Be careful the glue doesn't pass over onto the grain-side of the leather.

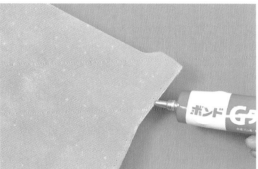

2 After the adhesive has dried, force a needle into one stitching hole (circled) and then feed it into the stitching hole (circled) on the opposite side.

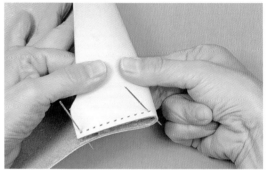

3 In order to prevent the glued edges from becoming crooked, pierce needles perpendicular to the surface and then gently press down on the leather.

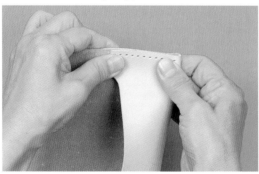

4 Every few stitches, make fine adjustments with a scratch awl to align the position of the stitching holes. Doing this will make stitching the leather easier.

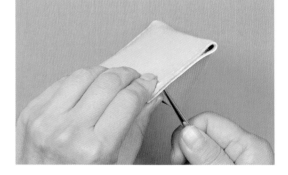

[Long and Wide Leather Piece]

Glue while sandwiching a piece of paper between the leather pieces to prevent glue spread. Pierce the stitching holes with a needle every few stitches as necessary to maintain alignment.
This is double-sided glue so it won't adhere if there is a piece of paper between the leather pieces.
Continue gluing while shifting the paper along bit by bit.

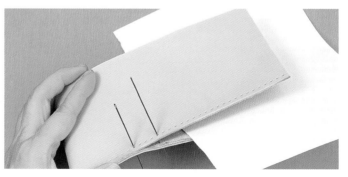

[Gluing of Gussets]

1 Lightly moisten the entire surface and slightly moisten the seam allowance.

2 Bend the seam allowance toward the grain-side.

3 Align the stitching holes marked with a circle on the gusset and main body. Temporarily fasten with thread. Glue the zones between the temporary fasteners. Apply glue to seam allowance, sandwich in some paper, and then slowly stick the two pieces together while aligning the stitching holes every few stitches.

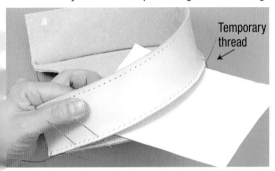

Temporary thread

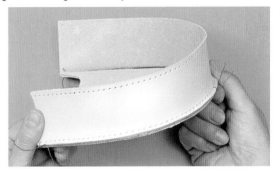

[Making 2-Ply Items]

1 One piece is cut according to the pattern – after punching stitching holes – while the other is roughly cut and oversized. Add glue to both sides and then press together.

2 Hold tightly while pressing down firmly with a slicker.

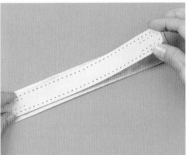
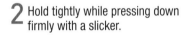
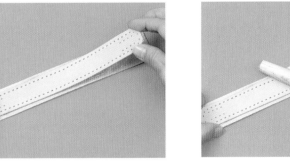

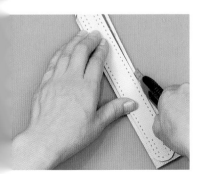
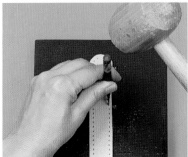

3 Place the piece, cut according to the pattern, face up and cut protruding leather edges so you are left with a single handle that matches the pattern.
Perforate the lower piece of leather using the upper stitching holes as a guide.
If the perforations refuse to penetrate completely, just turn the piece over and complete the hole from the back.

Preparing Thread and Needle

Leather sewing requires waxed thread. This type of thread resists thinning, which is essential due to the large amounts of friction produced in leathercrafting.

Thread must be waxed.

Waxed thread

Because it is waxed, this type of thread will easily collect dust. Prior to sewing, place your strand of thread on a piece of cloth, pinch it, and then pull to remove excess wax and impurities.

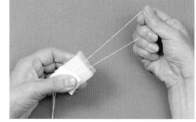

Wax block

Place one end of the thread on the wax, cover it with a cloth, and then pull the end and pass the thread over the wax while pressing down on the cloth. (Repeat 3-4 times)

[Length of Thread]

As a general guideline, use thread that is 4 times the length of the distance to be sewn.

Even if the sewing distance is short, make the thread a bit long for ease of use.

[Threading]

Since leather sewing requires one to continuously pull on the thread, you must use a special method to thread the needle so that the thread doesn't become loose.

★ For short distances, it's okay to leave the thread tip loose, just like when sewing fabric.

1 Thread through the needle (about twice the length of the needle itself).

2 Hold the thread. Loosen the twine of the thread by twisting it backward and then pierce the needle through the gaps a few times.

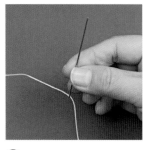 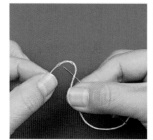 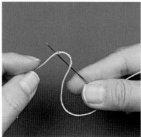 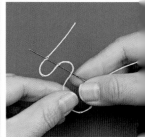

3 Push the point of the needle all the way through the thread.

4 Hold the longer thread and pull.

5 Adjust.

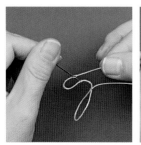 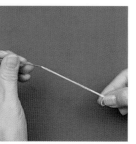 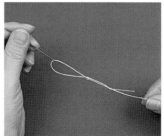 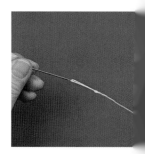

Decide where you will begin to stitch so that you finish at a point where finishing off thread ends is easy.

Adjust the left and right threads so that they are the same length.
★ For saddle stitching, thread one needle on each end.

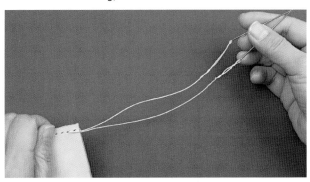

★ Thread that is too long is difficult to use. So, keep the length of each working thread to just under 1 m (3.28 ft.).

[Begin Stitching]

For bags, start stitching from the bottom so the stitch finishes at the opening. That way it will be easy to conceal the thread ends.

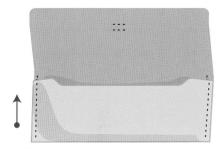

For small items, begin the stitch at the middle with a Running Stitch and come back to the middle.

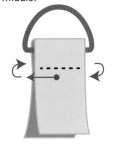

For long items where thread may run low while stitching (like handles, etc.), begin stitching from the middle.

[The First Stitch]

Initially pass the needle through a stitching hole that is a few holes from the end.

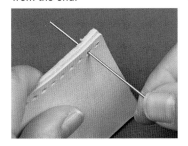

Double-stitch at the end.

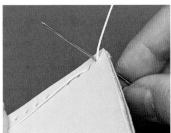

Come back to where it started.

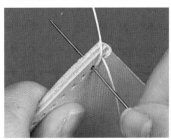

Since the openings of a bag or a pocket can easily become strained, always double stitch them at the ends.

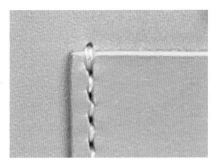

Saddle Stitch

This is the most common method of hand-stitching leather.

When stitching using two needles, firmly tighten the thread for each hole.
Even if one thread is cut the seam won't fray because it is sewn from both sides.

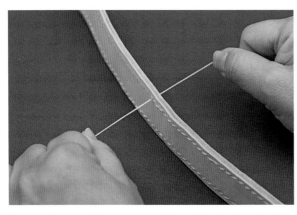

The saddle stitch is sturdy because both the left and right threads are firmly pulled as they go.

The photos use different colored thread to illustrate the instructions. One thread of each color is used.

1 Always start with the needle at the front side (red) first. Insert the needle in the first hole.

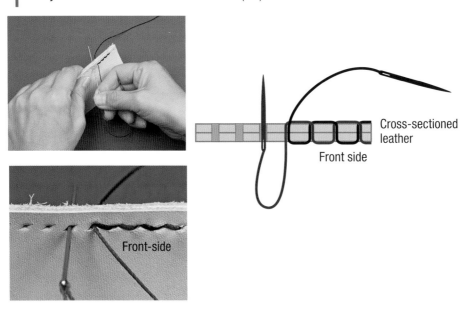

Cross-sectioned leather

Front side

Front-side

2 Pull the thread through at an angle (diagonally upward).

Widen the hole by pulling the thread through diagonally upward against the direction of the stitching.

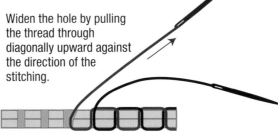

3 Insert the other needle (black) from the back-side into the same hole you just used.

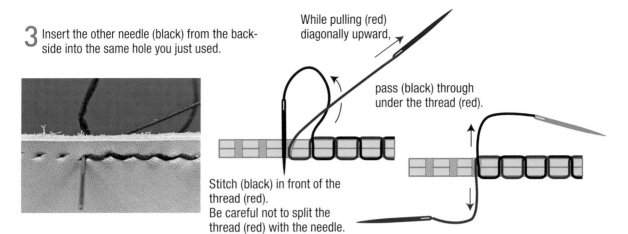

While pulling (red) diagonally upward,

pass (black) through under the thread (red).

Stitch (black) in front of the thread (red).
Be careful not to split the thread (red) with the needle.

4 Pull both threads at the same time.
For the next hole, insert the front-side needle into the hole and then, while pulling it diagonally upward, insert the back-side needle into the same hole. Doing so creates a beautiful finish stitch.

When a running stitch is doubled, it becomes a saddle stitch. Compared to a saddle stitch, the aesthetic of a running stitch is less appealing. However, it is suitable for sewing small items and thin leather whose shape would be deformed by forcefully pulling thread from both sides.

The photos use different colored thread to illustrate the instructions. One thread of each color is used.

Running Stitch

This is an easy stitch recommended for those who find saddle stitching difficult.

1 Thread a needle at one end. Adjust length so that the right side and left side are the same length.

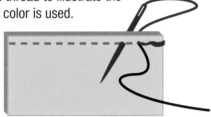

2 Begin to make a running stitch with one end of the thread.

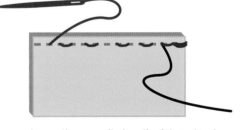

Leave the opposite length of thread as is.

3 After stitching is complete, pull the needle through to the back side and remove the needle. Thread the needle with the opposite side thread while being careful not to split the already stitched thread with the needle. Put the needle through the gap in the stitching hole and perform a running stitch all the way around.

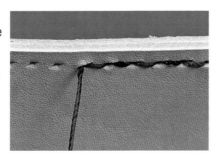

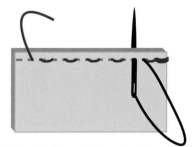

Begin stitching with the other thread.

[Splicing Thread]

1 When you run out of thread, backstitch once from the front side and pull the thread through to the back side. Then cut, but leave enough length to tie.
If continuing the stitch would make concealing the thread difficult, you can dispose of the thread at that position.

2 Thread a needle with some new thread and push it through the same hole where you made your last stitch. Continue to sew.

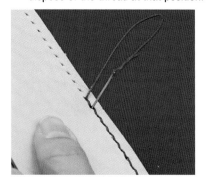
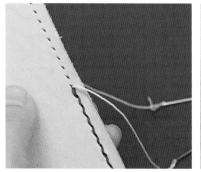
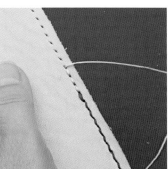

Ending Stitching and Dealing with Thread Ends

Conceal thread ends where they will not be obviously noticed. For example, you can hide the ends inside of a bag or on the back side of an item like a handle.
Apply woodworking glue on the stitching hole to seal. DO NOT apply glue to the thread.
Use a needle or hole punch to apply glue to the stitching hole.

1 A few stitches before the stitch ends, leave a tail of thread on the back side. Then, stitch using the other needle to the end.

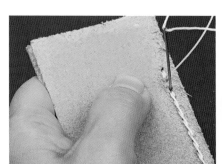

2 Stitch twice at the end, and then stitch back to a few stitches behind the tail of the thread.

[Tying the Thread as a Finishing Method]

1 Place woodworking glue over the stitching hole you wish to close.

2 Tie tightly again by pulling firmly on the threads. Push the thread ends down with a hole punch.

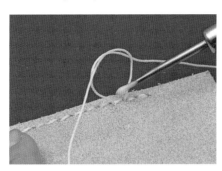
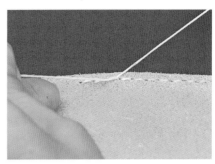

[Cut the Thread to Finish]

Cut thread ends just a little long.

If the thread will be too visible, cut it after reverse stitching through the other side. Apply glue to several stitching holes, both before and after the trimmed threads. Press the ends into the leather and glue firmly.

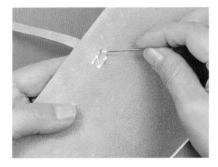

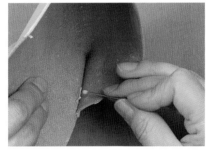

After reverse stitching to the inside of a bag, cut the thread relatively short to conceal thread ends.
Apply glue to tip of needle. Glue several stitching holes, both before and after the finishing stitch. Press thread down firmly with a scratch awl, etc.

[Adjusting Seams]

Striking the seams with a mallet will align the threads and make them sit better in the leather.

Stitching Steps

Order depends on what is being made.

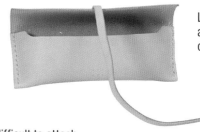

Like with the basic pen case, parts attached to the flap side can be sewn on after the main body is complete.

For components and metal fittings that are difficult to attach after the main body is complete, polish their edges and attach before the main body is put together.

Attach a snap fastener to main body before sewing.

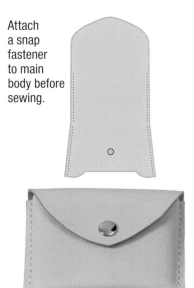

Attach pieces before sewing main body.

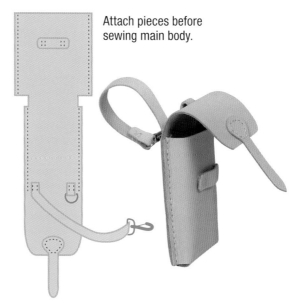

Attach zippcr before sewing the main body.

Adjust the position of the flap after sewing and then attach the metal fitting

The handle is basically attached before the main body is sewn.

Sew the handle, leaving off the ends where it will be attached to the main body.

Now sew the left off ends to the main body side.

The handle on this bag is obviously attached after the main body is sewn.

Adjust the seam allowance after sewing.
If you first inflate a flat object – like the basic pen case – it will be easier to put items in or remove them.

[Inflating]

1 Lightly moisten the entire grain-side surface with a sponge soaked in water and wrung out. Spread the seams with a slicker.

2 Insert some folded up newspaper, or something similar. The corners of the newspaper that reach the bottom should be rounded so as not to stretch out the bottom of the case too much.

[Polishing the Edge]

1 Use a dresser to flatten any uneven seam allowances.

2 Apply Tokonole to the edge.

3 Polish with leather scraps. Repeating steps 1, 2, and 3 will cause the edge to become glossy.

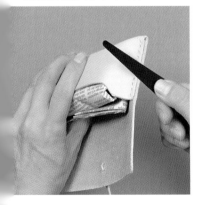

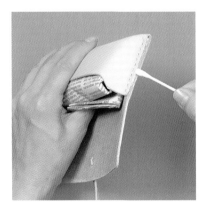

[Applying Oil]

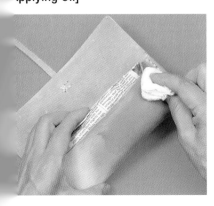

Applying leather oil will produce a natural feel and prevent mold.

Put some on a soft cloth and apply thinly and carefully.

The basic pen case is complete!

CHAPTER 5

Patterns

About the Patterns

★ The enlargement scale for photocopying is 160%.
Photocopy each page on 11" x 17" (ledger size) paper.

★ When multiples of a component are needed, the number of pieces required is specified.
Otherwise, produce one pattern per diagram.

★ The finished size for each project is only approximate. Finished sizes may vary slightly
depending on leather thickness and finishing methods.

★ After enlarging to 160% scale, metal fittings become close to actual size.

A dot denotes the position for punching each hole.

When punching, align the center of the hole punch with the center of the dot.

★ Dashed lines are drawn on the pattern approximately where hooks, latches, and other fittings
should be placed after stitching. Mark their positions after confirming on your working project.

Refer to pp. 76 ~ 79 when sizing snap
fasteners, rivets, or grommets.

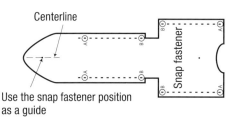

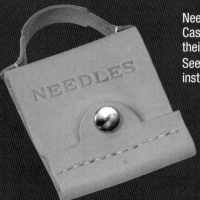

Needle and Wax Block
Case, from p. 114, with
their flaps fastened.
See Chapter 5 for
instructions.

Open Fully

Book

To prevent distortion, be sure to hold the book's pages firmly open when making your pattern photocopies.

Chapter 5 Table of Contents

Attaching Zippers	138
Altering Pattern Sizes	139
Constructing the Pattern (Flat Bag)	140
Needle and Wax Block Case	190
Leather Fortune Cookie	191
When the Stitching Holes Are Misaligned	191

Chapter 1

Card Case	142
Simple Smartphone Holder	142
Simple Document Case	142
Notebook Cover	144
Earphone and Cord Case	145
Mask Bag	146
Medicine and Bandage Case	147
Cases for Cosmetics and Candy	149
Envelope-Shaped Document Holder	150
Simple Clutch Bag	151
Zipper Pouch and Pen Case	153
Tall Tote Bag	154
Boxy-Bottom Shoulder Bag	156
Box-Shaped Clutch Bag	159
Box-Shaped USB Case	161
Box-Shaped Pen Case and Business Card Case	162
Box-Shaped Smartphone Holder	163
Pouch with Darts	165
Glasses Case	166
Boxed-Corner Small Pouch (Top)	167
Boxed-Corner Small Pouch (Bottom)	168

Accessory Case	169
Plastic Bottle Holder	169

Chapter 2

"Stenciling" Flat Pouch	152+173
"Stitch on Flesh-Side and Turn Inside-Out" Pouch	153
"Various Types of Tanned Leather" Drawstring Bag	170
"Dyeing with Liquid Dye" Name Tag	171
"Indigo Dye on Leather" Pen Case	172
"Embossing" Clipboard	172
"Dyeing with Markers" Charm	173
"Edge Dyeing" Key Chain	173
"Stenciling" Flat Pouch (Large)	173
Buckles and Straps	174

Chapter 3

Binoculars Case	175
Bottom-Gusset Clutch Bag	176
Bicolor Tote Bag	177
Round-Bottom Shoulder Bag	179
Small Bag with Handles	181
Round Bag	183
Square Bag	184
Satchel-Style Bag	186
Drawstring Bag	189

Make sure this gauge size is correct on each photocopied pattern. Unit of Measurement cm

10

0

Patterns in Chapter 5 are printed away from the spine in order to make photocopying easy. For that reason, page numbers are printed on the inside edge of each page.

Attaching Zippers

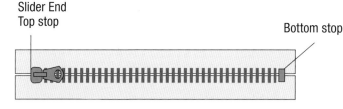

Slider End
Top stop

Bottom stop

[Zipper Size]

The zipper size is the length from the top stop to the bottom stop.

There are stores that will adjust the zipper length if you need non-standard sizes.

[Attaching a Zipper to an Opening]

1 Apply glue – in a narrow line – along outer edge of seam allowance on flesh-side.

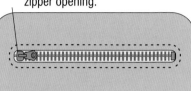

2 Bond the zipper in such a way that the top stop fits snugly in the zipper opening.

3 Glue both tape ends by folding them. This will prevent the tape ends from accidentally covering the zipper teeth.

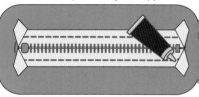

[Attaching a Zipper to Front and Back Pieces]

1 Apply glue – in a narrow line – along outer edge of seam allowance on flesh-side.

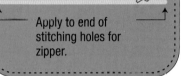

Apply to end of stitching holes for zipper.

2 Bond zipper while placing the top stop inside of the stitching hole limits.

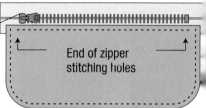

End of zipper stitching holes

3 Align attached leather piece with the opposite leather piece.

Ruler

4 Fold in the tape ends and glue. This will prevent them from covering the teeth of the zipper.

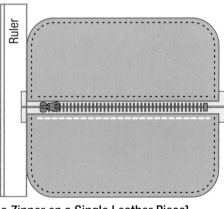

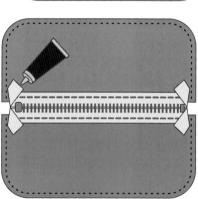

[Attaching a Zipper on a Single Leather Piece]

1 Apply glue – in a narrow line – along outer edge of seam allowance on the flesh-side.

End of zipper stitching holes

2 Attach one side of the zipper.
Lightly mark position of the leather edge.

End of zipper stitching holes
Bond zipper while placing the top stop inside of the stitching hole limits.

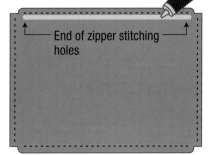

3 Line up the mark on the zipper tape with the edge of the leather and attach. If you don't attach zipper tabs, just fold the tape ends in and glue them.

This section lays out methods for altering pattern sizes.
If there are few components, and the stitching holes are straight, you can easily change the size by cutting and repasting the pattern to the desired length.
Paste the cut patterns on graph paper (5 mm / ¼ in. x 5 mm / ¼ in.) to help alter their size.
The rule for altering pattern sizes is to modify by 5 mm / ¼ in. where stitching holes exist because stitching hole intervals are 5 mm / ¼ in.

[Altering Areas without Stitching holes]

Box-Shaped Smartphone Holder

Expand the width

Flaps that don't have stitching holes can be altered freely.

Pattern

Do not move marks or stitching holes located at center.

Split the pattern and move the right and left sides evenly away from the center.

[Altering Areas with Stitching Holes]

Simple Smartphone Holder

Pattern

Alter size by 5 mm / ¼ in.
Add stitching holes in 5 mm / ¼ in. intervals.

★ If there are stitching holes or marks in the center, cut the pattern while leaving the center as in the example.

If there are two ○ side by side, separate evenly with 5 mm / ¼ in. between the marks. Add stitching holes in 5 mm / ¼ in. intervals.

[Altering Gusset Width]

Binoculars Case

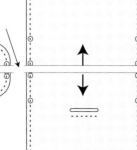

Pattern

★ Altering the size is more challenging if the pattern is more complex than the examples given here.

Constructing the Pattern

Large-sized patterns that do not fit on a single page are divided.

Make as many enlarged photocopies as required and put them together by pasting on large-sized paper.

160%

[Flat Bag, p. 18]

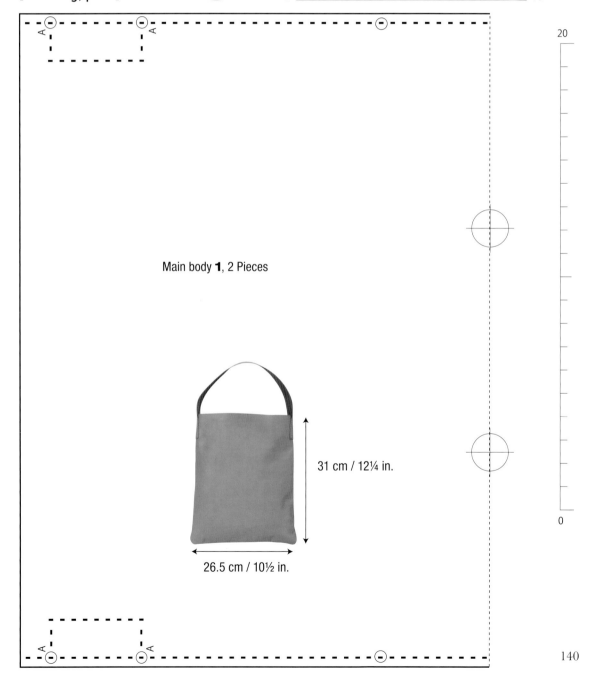

Main body **1**

Photocopied pattern

Cut the photocopied pattern along the dotted line and paste it on a piece of simili paper.

Simili paper

0 ⌞_____⌟ 10

20

Main body **1**, 2 Pieces

31 cm / 12¼ in.

26.5 cm / 10½ in.

0

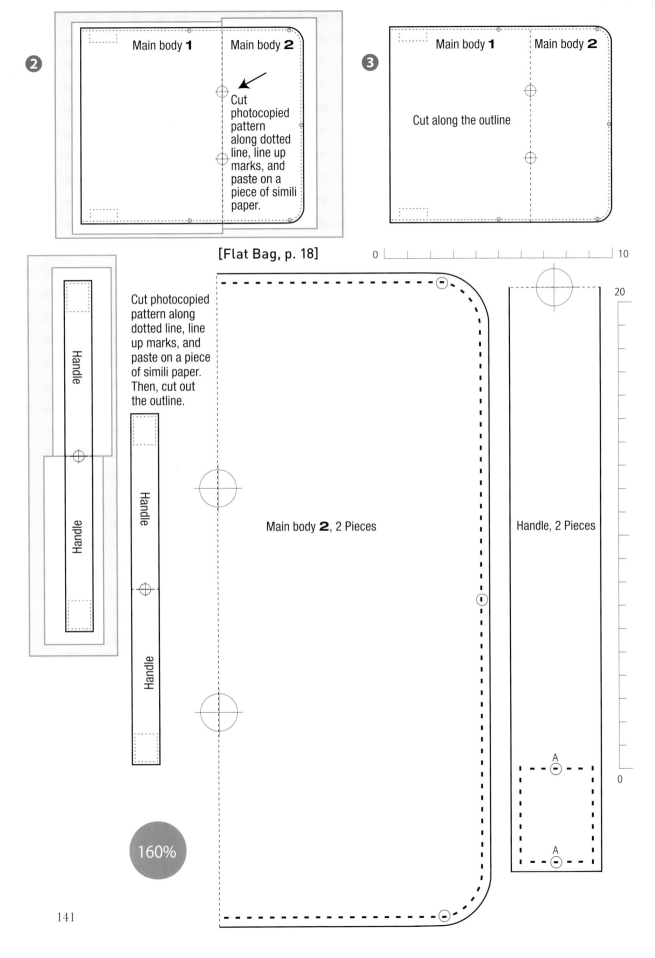

② Main body **1**   Main body **2**

Cut photocopied pattern along dotted line, line up marks, and paste on a piece of simili paper.

③ Main body **1**   Main body **2**

Cut along the outline

[Flat Bag, p. 18]

0 |_____| 10

Handle
Handle

Cut photocopied pattern along dotted line, line up marks, and paste on a piece of simili paper. Then, cut out the outline.

Handle
Handle
Handle

Main body **2**, 2 Pieces

Handle, 2 Pieces

A

A

20

0

160%

141

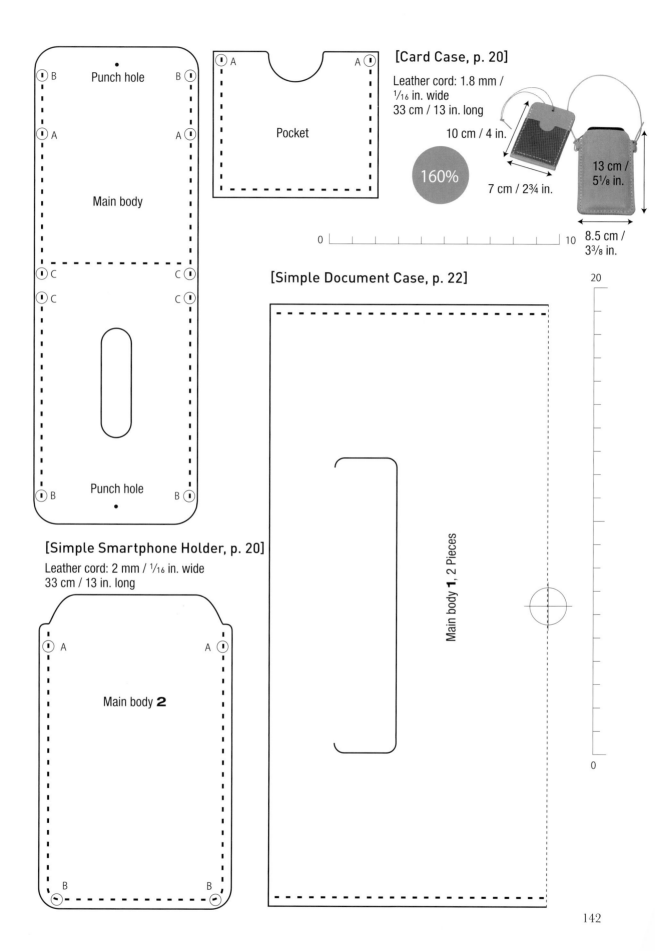

Punch hole

B

A

Main body

C

C

B

Punch hole

A

Pocket

A

[Card Case, p. 20]

Leather cord: 1.8 mm /
¹/₁₆ in. wide
33 cm / 13 in. long

10 cm / 4 in.

160%

7 cm / 2¾ in.

13 cm /
5¹/₈ in.

0 ⌊_____⌋ 10

8.5 cm /
3³/₈ in.

[Simple Document Case, p. 22]

20

Main body **1**, 2 Pieces

[Simple Smartphone Holder, p. 20]

Leather cord: 2 mm / ¹/₁₆ in. wide
33 cm / 13 in. long

A

A

Main body 2

B

B

0

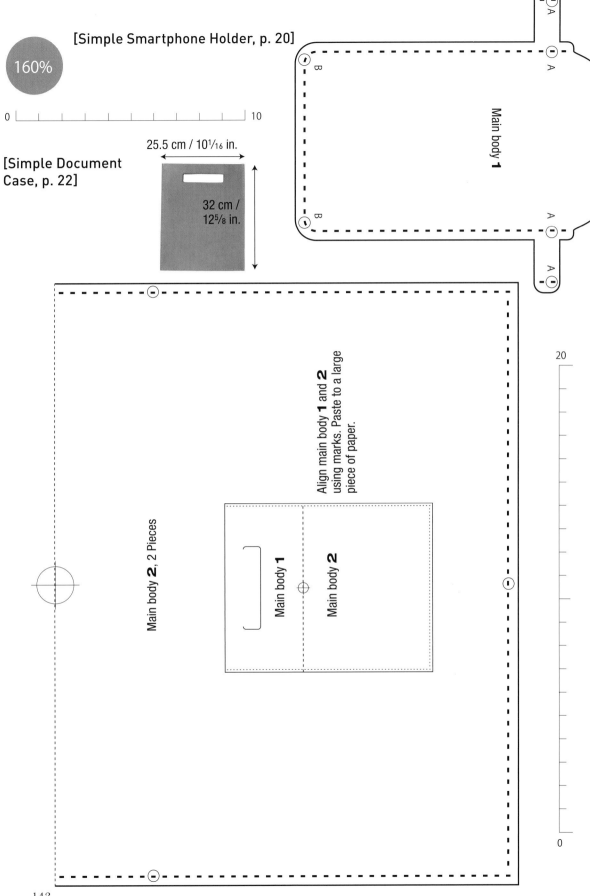

[Simple Smartphone Holder, p. 20]

160%

0 ⌊_____⌋ 10

[Simple Document Case, p. 22]

25.5 cm / 10 1/16 in.

32 cm / 12 5/8 in.

Main body **1**

B   A

B   A

A

A

Main body **2**, 2 Pieces

Align main body **1** and **2** using marks. Paste to a large piece of paper.

Main body **1**

Main body **2**

20

0

143

0 |___|___|___|___|___|___|___|___|___|___| 10

160%

Snap fastener

Main body

20

A

B

A

B

A

B

Pocket 1

Pocket 2

Snap fastener

Belt

17 cm /
6¾ in.

11.5 cm /
4½ in.

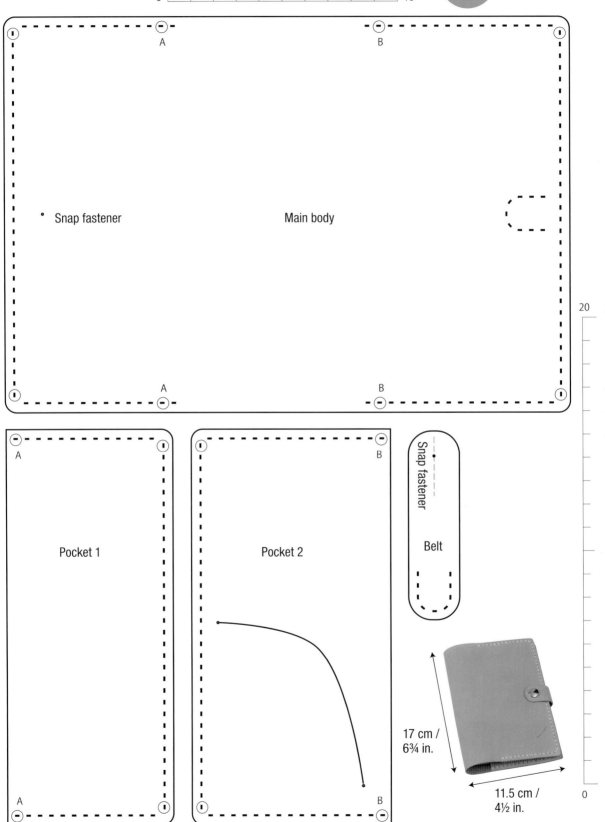

0

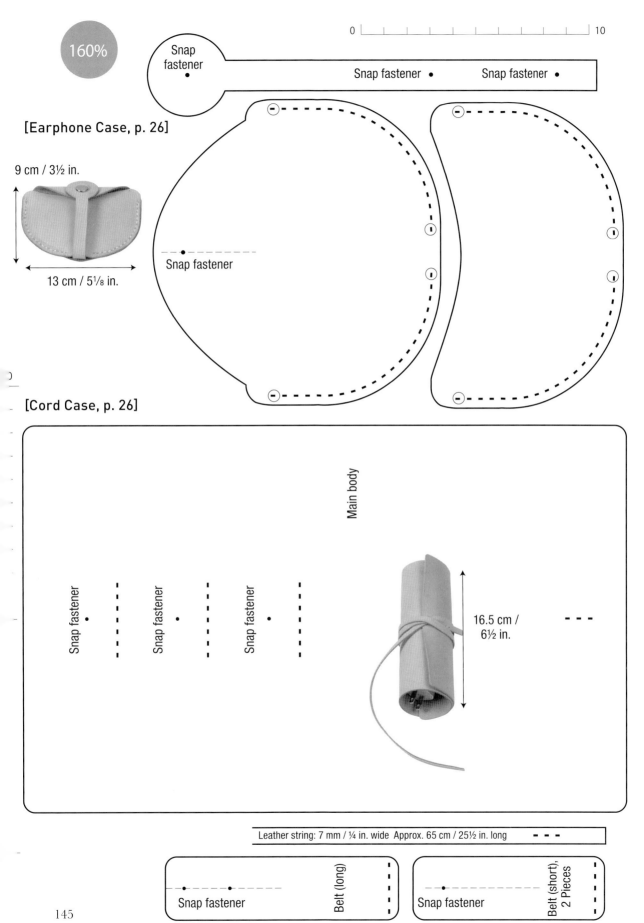

160%

0 |_____| 10

Snap fastener

Snap fastener •   Snap fastener •

[Earphone Case, p. 26]

9 cm / 3½ in.

13 cm / 5⅛ in.

Snap fastener

[Cord Case, p. 26]

Main body

Snap fastener •

Snap fastener •

Snap fastener •

16.5 cm / 6½ in.

Leather string: 7 mm / ¼ in. wide Approx. 65 cm / 25½ in. long - - -

Snap fastener   Belt (long)

Snap fastener   Belt (short), 2 Pieces

145

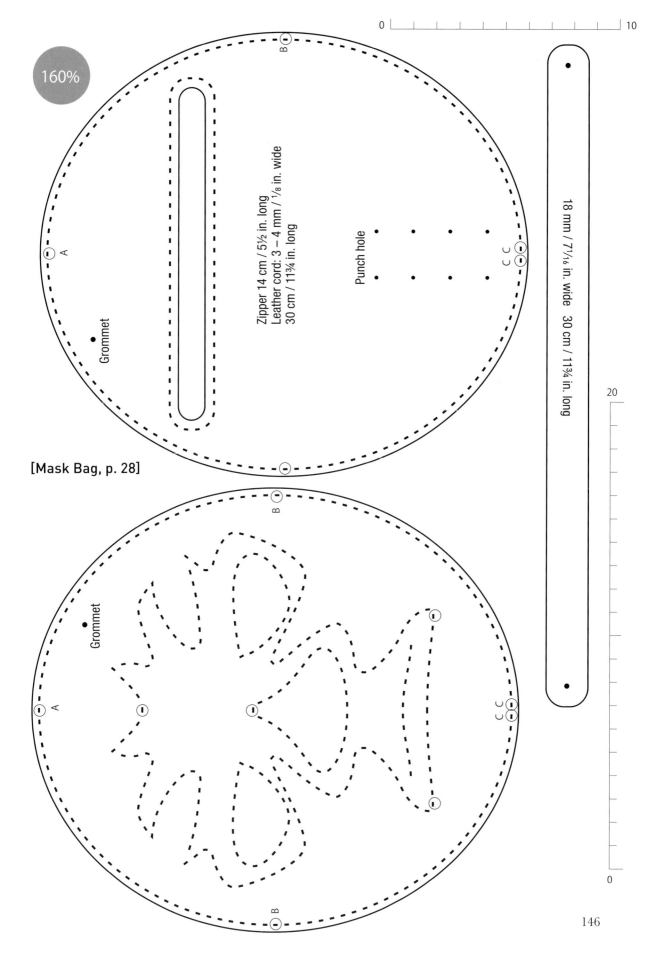

160%

[Mask Bag, p. 28]

0 —————————— 10

B

A

Grommet

Zipper 14 cm / 5½ in. long
Leather cord: 3 – 4 mm / ⅛ in. wide
30 cm / 11¾ in. long

Punch hole

C C

18 mm / 7¹⁄₁₆ in. wide 30 cm / 11¾ in. long

20

B

Grommet

A

C C

B

0

146

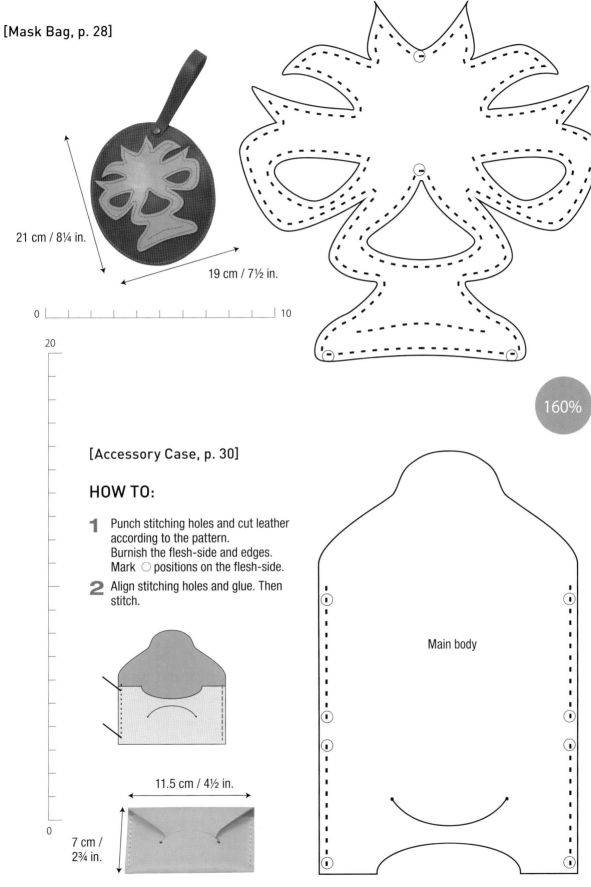

[Mask Bag, p. 28]

21 cm / 8¼ in.

19 cm / 7½ in.

0 ⌞_____⌟ 10

160%

20

[Accessory Case, p. 30]

HOW TO:

1 Punch stitching holes and cut leather according to the pattern.
Burnish the flesh-side and edges.
Mark ○ positions on the flesh-side.

2 Align stitching holes and glue. Then stitch.

11.5 cm / 4½ in.

7 cm / 2¾ in.

Main body

147

[Medicine and Bandage Case, p. 30]

0 |_____| 10

160%

HOW TO:

The size is different but the production steps are the same.

1 Punch stitching holes and cut leather according to the pattern.
Burnish the flesh-side and edges.
Mark ○ positions on the flesh-side.

2 Refer to the pattern to align stitching holes on case front, case back, and flap fastener. Then, glue.

3 Begin stitching.

Bandage Case
Leather cord: approx.
30 – 40 cm /
11¾ in. – 15¾ in.

6 cm / 2⅜ in.

9 cm / 3½ in.

Medicine Case
Leather cord: approx. 40 – 50 cm /
15¾ in. – 19¾ in.

20

0

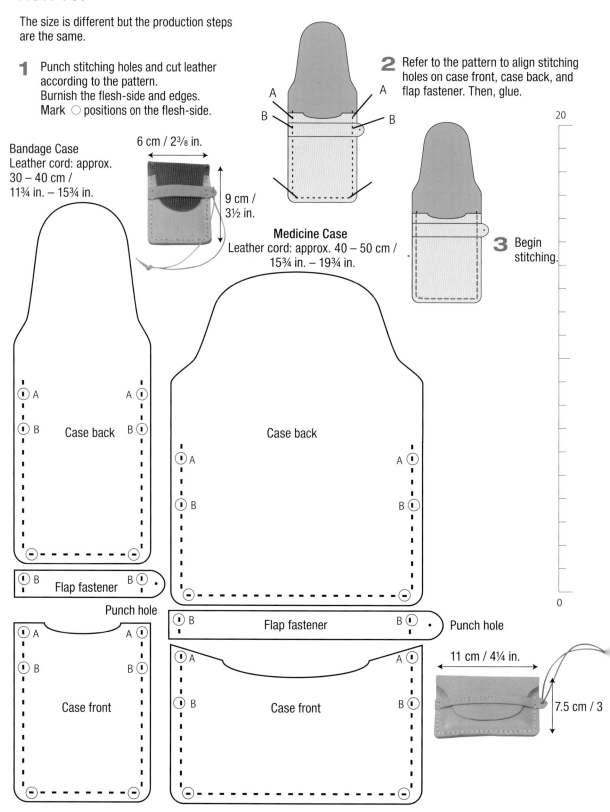

A
B
Case back
A
B

Case back

A
B

A
B

⊙ B Flap fastener B ⊙ •

Punch hole

⊙ B Flap fastener B ⊙ • Punch hole

A
B
Case front
A
B

A
B
Case front
A
B

11 cm / 4¼ in.

7.5 cm / 3

148

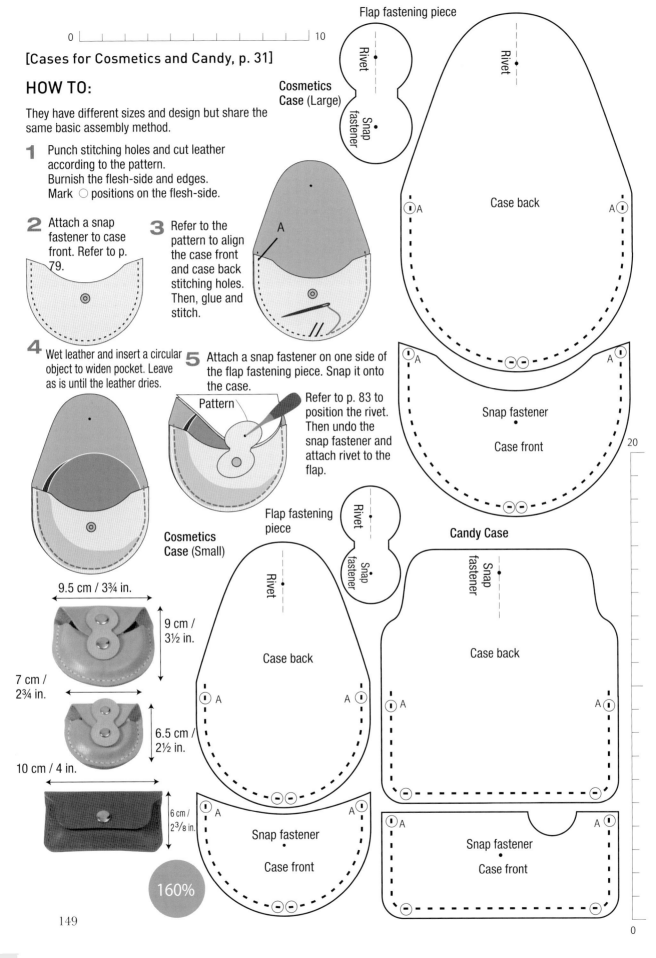

Flap fastening piece

Cosmetics Case (Large)

Rivet

Rivet

Snap fastener

[Cases for Cosmetics and Candy, p. 31]

0 _____ 10

HOW TO:

They have different sizes and design but share the same basic assembly method.

1 Punch stitching holes and cut leather according to the pattern.
Burnish the flesh-side and edges.
Mark ○ positions on the flesh-side.

2 Attach a snap fastener to case front. Refer to p. 79.

3 Refer to the pattern to align the case front and case back stitching holes. Then, glue and stitch.

A

4 Wet leather and insert a circular object to widen pocket. Leave as is until the leather dries.

5 Attach a snap fastener on one side of the flap fastening piece. Snap it onto the case.

Pattern

Refer to p. 83 to position the rivet. Then undo the snap fastener and attach rivet to the flap.

Case back

A   A

A   A

Snap fastener

Case front

20

Flap fastening piece

Rivet

Snap fastener

Candy Case

Rivet

Snap fastener

Cosmetics Case (Small)

Case back

A   A

A   A

Case back

A   A

9.5 cm / 3¾ in.

9 cm / 3½ in.

7 cm / 2¾ in.

6.5 cm / 2½ in.

10 cm / 4 in.

6 cm / 2⅜ in.

160%

Snap fastener

Case front

A   A

Snap fastener

Case front

149

[Envelope-Shaped Document Case, p. 32]

Leather cord: 5 mm / ¼ in. wide
40 cm / 15¾ in. long

String stopper piece

Punch stitching holes and cut out the two string stopper pieces. Make each string stopper 2-ply by gluing on a separate leather piece.

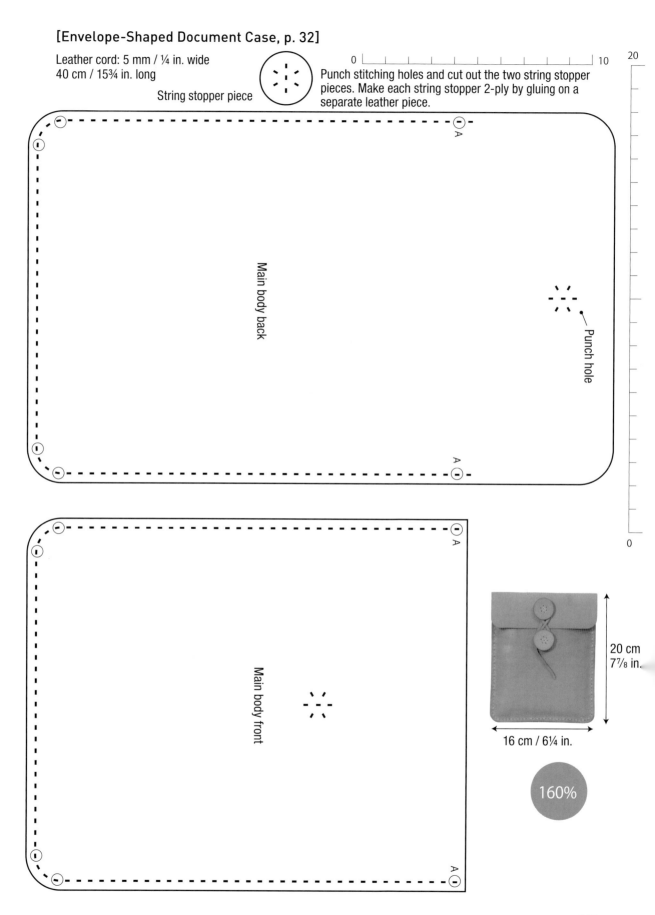

Main body back

Punch hole

A

A

Main body front

A

A

20 cm
7⅞ in.

16 cm / 6¼ in.

160%

0 | | | | | | | | | | 10

160%

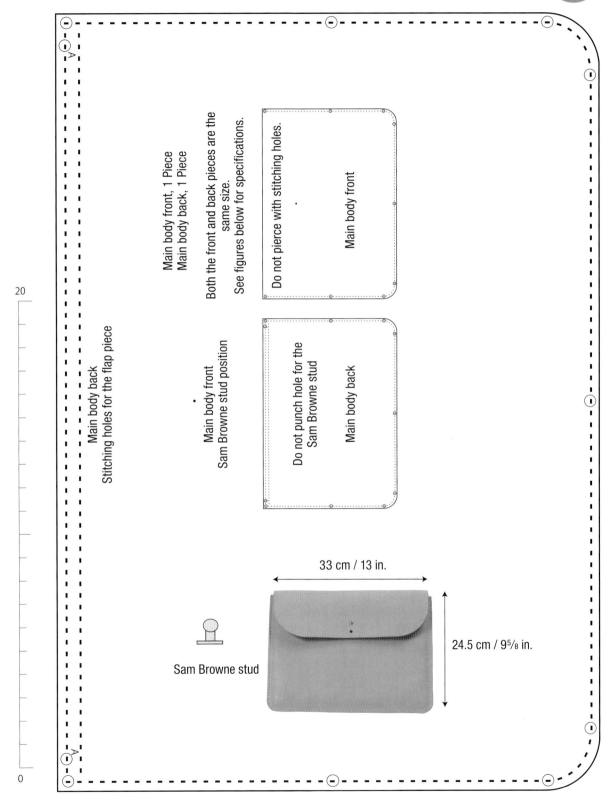

Main body front, 1 Piece
Main body back, 1 Piece

Both the front and back pieces are the same size.
See figures below for specifications.

Do not pierce with stitching holes.

Main body front

Main body front
Sam Browne stud position

Do not punch hole for the Sam Browne stud

Main body back

Main body back
Stitching holes for the flap piece

20

33 cm / 13 in.

24.5 cm / 9⅝ in.

Sam Browne stud

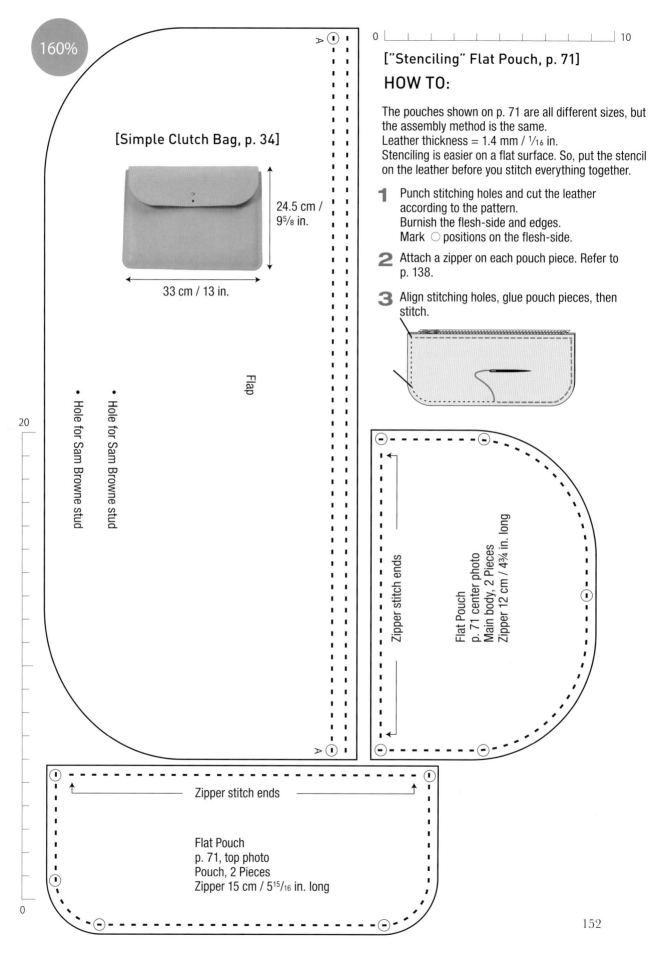

160%

[Simple Clutch Bag, p. 34]

24.5 cm / 9⅝ in.

33 cm / 13 in.

A

Flap

• Hole for Sam Browne stud
• Hole for Sam Browne stud

20

A

["Stenciling" Flat Pouch, p. 71]

HOW TO:

The pouches shown on p. 71 are all different sizes, but the assembly method is the same.
Leather thickness = 1.4 mm / 1/16 in.
Stenciling is easier on a flat surface. So, put the stencil on the leather before you stitch everything together.

1 Punch stitching holes and cut the leather according to the pattern.
Burnish the flesh-side and edges.
Mark ○ positions on the flesh-side.

2 Attach a zipper on each pouch piece. Refer to p. 138.

3 Align stitching holes, glue pouch pieces, then stitch.

Zipper stitch ends

Flat Pouch
p. 71 center photo
Main body, 2 Pieces
Zipper 12 cm / 4¾ in. long

Zipper stitch ends

Flat Pouch
p. 71, top photo
Pouch, 2 Pieces
Zipper 15 cm / 5¹⁵/₁₆ in. long

0

152

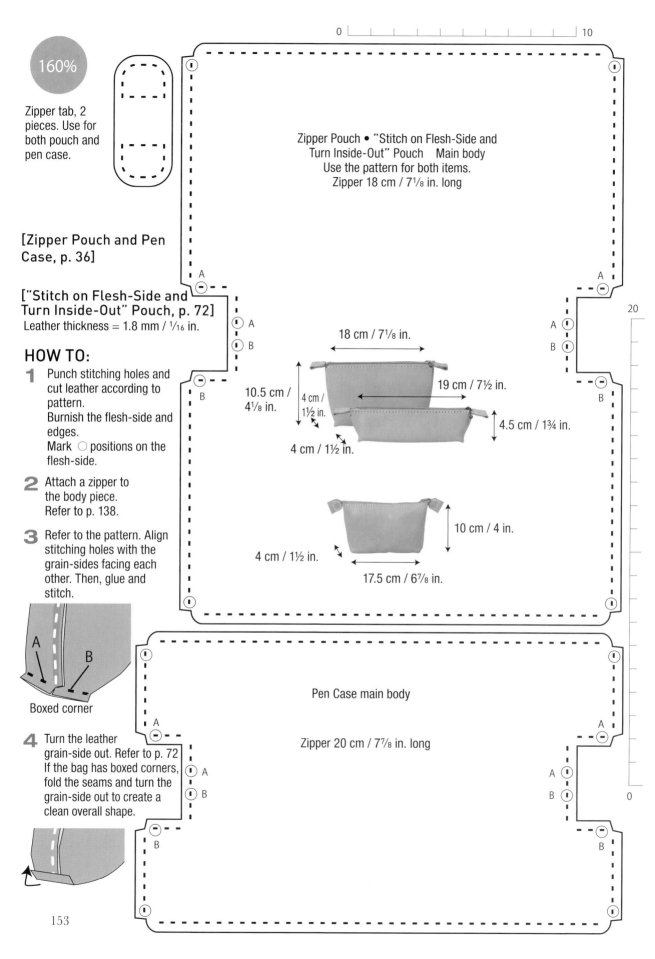

160%

Zipper tab, 2 pieces. Use for both pouch and pen case.

Zipper Pouch • "Stitch on Flesh-Side and Turn Inside-Out" Pouch   Main body
Use the pattern for both items.
Zipper 18 cm / 7⅛ in. long

[Zipper Pouch and Pen Case, p. 36]

["Stitch on Flesh-Side and Turn Inside-Out" Pouch, p. 72]
Leather thickness = 1.8 mm / ¹/₁₆ in.

HOW TO:

1 Punch stitching holes and cut leather according to pattern.
Burnish the flesh-side and edges.
Mark ○ positions on the flesh-side.

2 Attach a zipper to the body piece.
Refer to p. 138.

3 Refer to the pattern. Align stitching holes with the grain-sides facing each other. Then, glue and stitch.

A   B

Boxed corner

4 Turn the leather grain-side out. Refer to p. 72
If the bag has boxed corners, fold the seams and turn the grain-side out to create a clean overall shape.

18 cm / 7⅛ in.

19 cm / 7½ in.

10.5 cm / 4⅛ in.

4 cm / 1½ in.

4 cm / 1½ in.

4.5 cm / 1¾ in.

10 cm / 4 in.

4 cm / 1½ in.

17.5 cm / 6⅞ in.

Pen Case main body

Zipper 20 cm / 7⅞ in. long

A
B

A
B

A
B

A
B

A
B

A
B

0   10   20   0

153

0 |___|___|___|___|___|___|___|___|___|___| 10

Main body **1**, 2 Pieces

A

31 cm /
12¼ in.

5 cm /
2 in.

21.5 cm / 8½ in.

Handle **1**, 2 Pieces

[Tall Tote Bag, p. 38]

0 |___|___|___|___|___|___|___|___|___|___| 10

B Ⓘ

Ⓘ C

B Ⓘ   C Ⓘ

Main body **2**

For both main body and handle pieces: Align marks and paste to a large piece of paper.

Main body **1**	Main body **2**	Main body **1**

Handle **1**	⊕	Handle **2**

Ⓘ B   Ⓘ C

B Ⓘ   C Ⓘ

Handle **2**, 2 Pieces

A Ⓘ

Ⓘ

Ⓘ

A Ⓘ

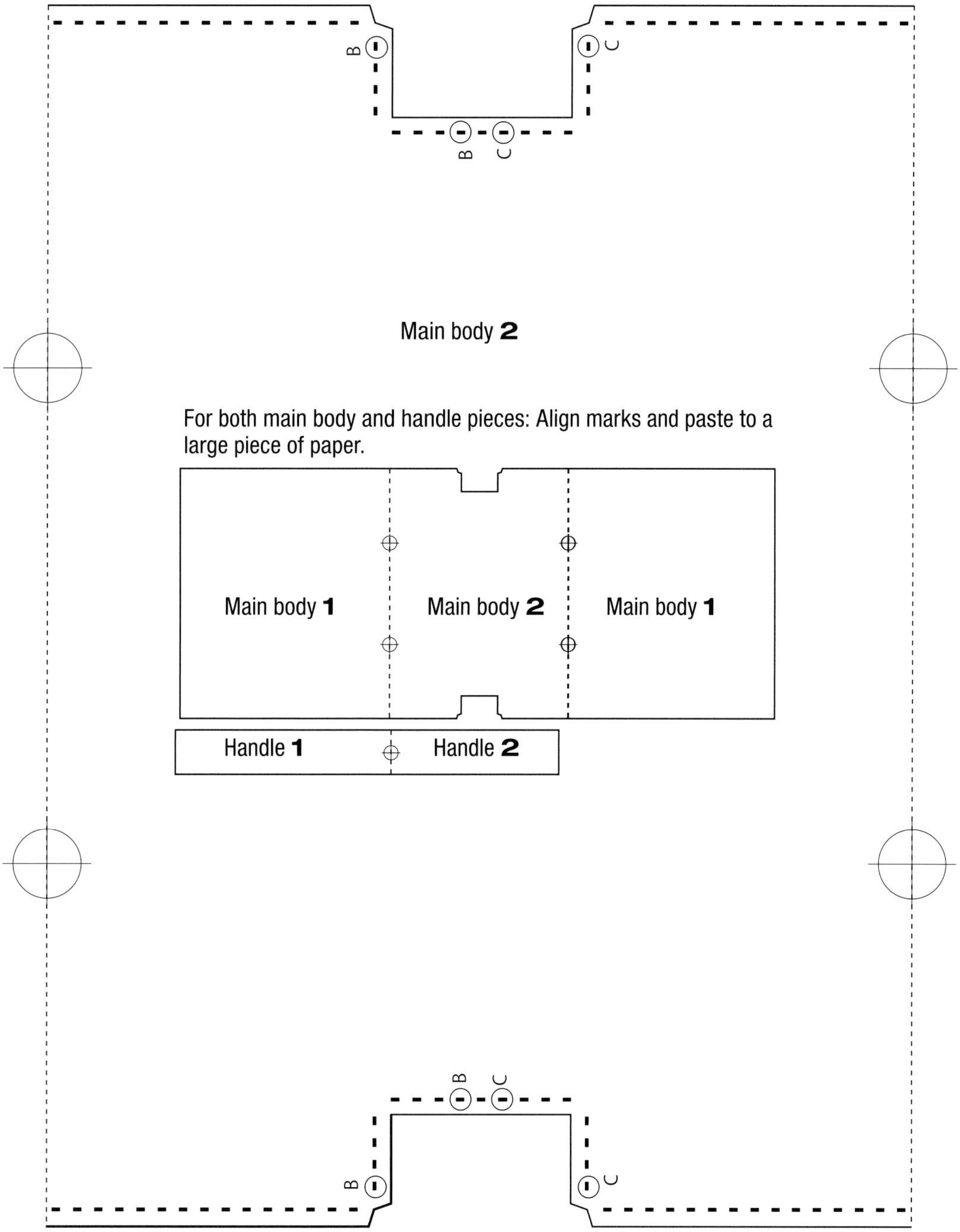

[Boxy-Bottom Shoulder Bag, p. 40]

See p. 74 for the strap pattern and instructions

160%

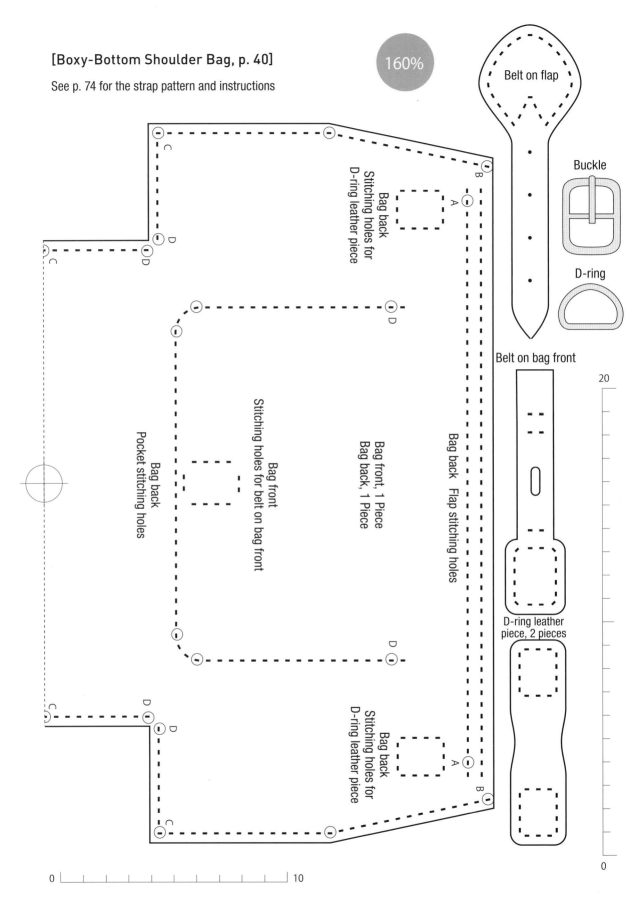

Belt on flap

Buckle

D-ring

Belt on bag front

D-ring leather piece, 2 pieces

Bag back
Stitching holes for
D-ring leather piece

A

B

C

D

Bag back
Pocket stitching holes

Bag front
Stitching holes for belt on bag front

Bag front, 1 Piece
Bag back, 1 Piece

Bag back Flap stitching holes

20

0 |_____| 10

0

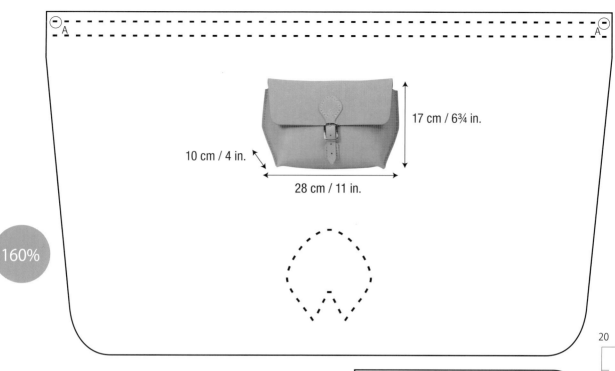

160%

17 cm / 6¾ in.

10 cm / 4 in.

28 cm / 11 in.

[Folded-Bottom Shoulder Bag, p. 40]

Front and back pieces are the same size.
Make two photocopies of the pattern and put
them together as seen in the figure below.

Front side

Back side

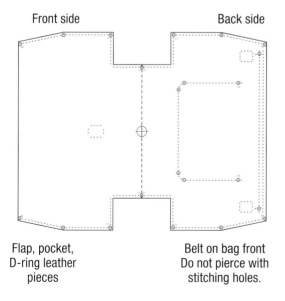

Flap, pocket,
D-ring leather
pieces

Belt on bag front
Do not pierce with
stitching holes.

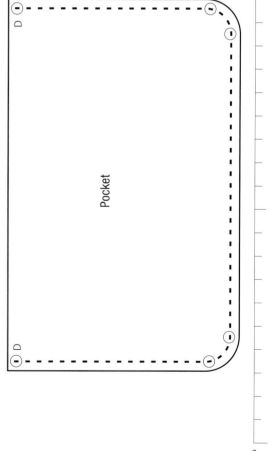

Pocket

20

0

0   10

[Folded-Bottom Shoulder Bag, p. 40]

HOW TO:

1 Punch stitching holes and cut leather according to the pattern.
Burnish the flesh-side and edges.
Mark ○ positions on the flesh-side.

2 Pass buckle through belt on bag front piece and fold in half. Align stitching holes on both ends of belt piece. Glue and stitch as shown in the figure at left.
Put D-ring leather piece through D-ring and fold the leather piece in half. Align stitching holes on both ends of leather piece and glue together. Refer to p. 85.

3 Refer to the pattern to align the stitching holes. Glue required components on the bag and then stitch them on.

4 Fold the bag piece. Refer to the pattern and align the stitching holes from B to C (figure below). Then, glue and stitch.

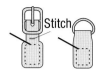

Stitch

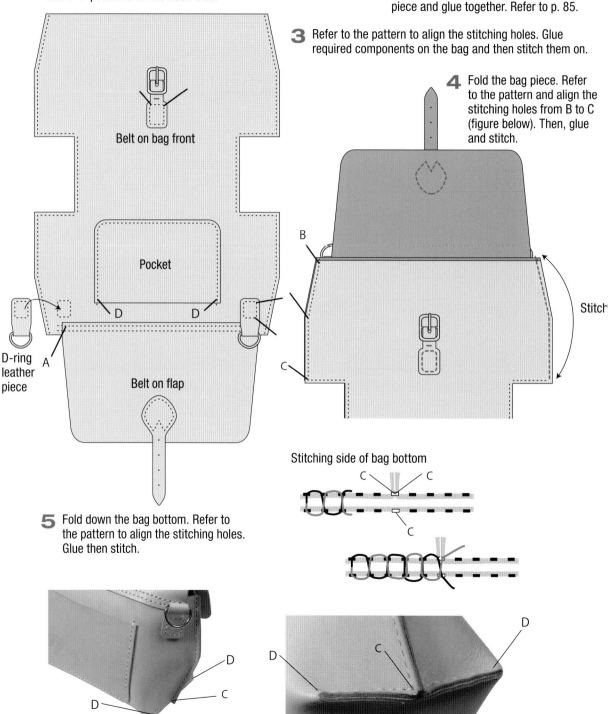

Belt on bag front

Pocket

D   D

D-ring leather piece

A

Belt on flap

B

C

Stitch

5 Fold down the bag bottom. Refer to the pattern to align the stitching holes. Glue then stitch.

Stitching side of bag bottom

C   C

C

D

D

C

D

D   C

Bag bottom

160%

0 |_____| 10

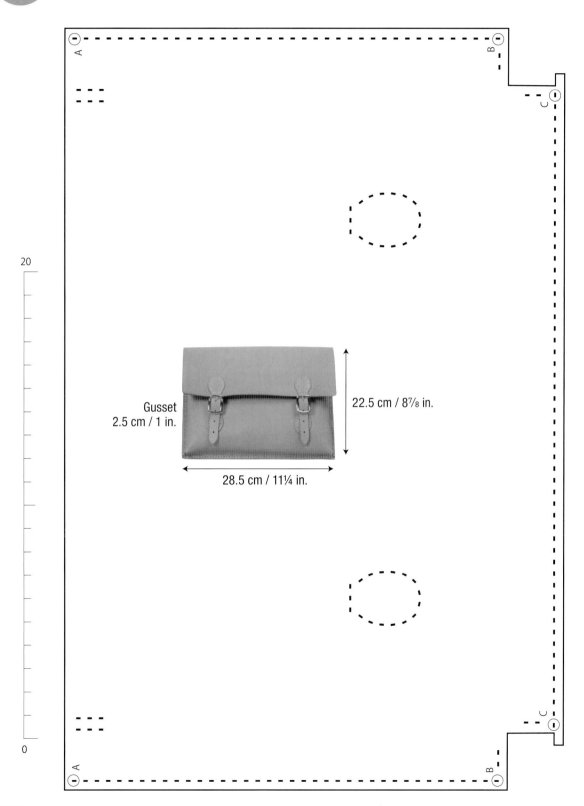

20

Gusset
2.5 cm / 1 in.

22.5 cm / 8⅞ in.

28.5 cm / 11¼ in.

0

0 |⌐_____| 10

160%

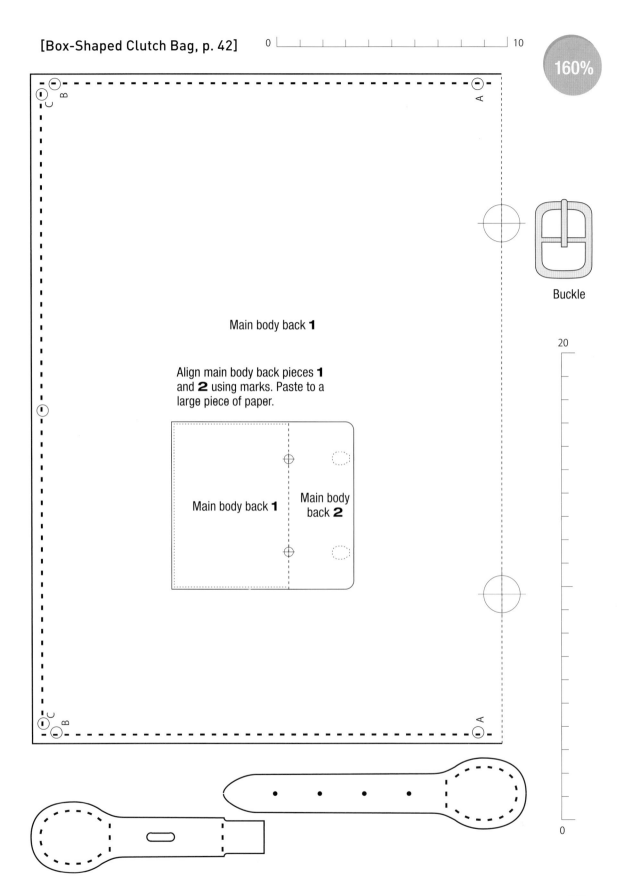

Buckle

Main body back **1**

Align main body back pieces **1** and **2** using marks. Paste to a large piece of paper.

Main body back **1**

Main body back **2**

20

0

[Box-Shaped Clutch Bag, p. 42]

160%

20

Main body back **2**

0

0 |⎯⎯⎯⎯⎯⎯⎯⎯⎯⎯⎯| 10

Each USB device has a different shape.
Cut out pattern and then place the USB
device on the pattern to adjust flap length.

[Box-Shaped USB Case, p. 44]

HOW TO:

1 Punch stitching holes and cut leather
according to the pattern.
Burnish the flesh-side and edges.
Mark ○ positions on the flesh-side.

2
Attach a snap
fastener to the case
front. Refer to p. 79.
Moisten leather and
fold the case front,
gusset, and seam
allowance.

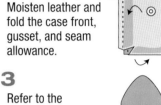

3
Refer to the
pattern when
aligning stitching
holes along the
side of the case.
Then, glue and
stitch.

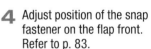

A
B

4 Adjust position of the snap
fastener on the flap front.
Refer to p. 83.

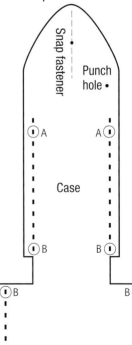

Snap fastener

Punch
hole •

A

A

Case

B

B

B

B

Snap fastener
•

A

A

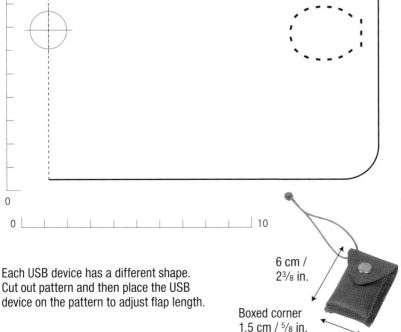

6 cm /
2³⁄₈ in.

Boxed corner
1.5 cm / ⁵⁄₈ in.

4 cm / 1½ in.

161

[Box-Shaped Pen Case, p. 44]

HOW TO:

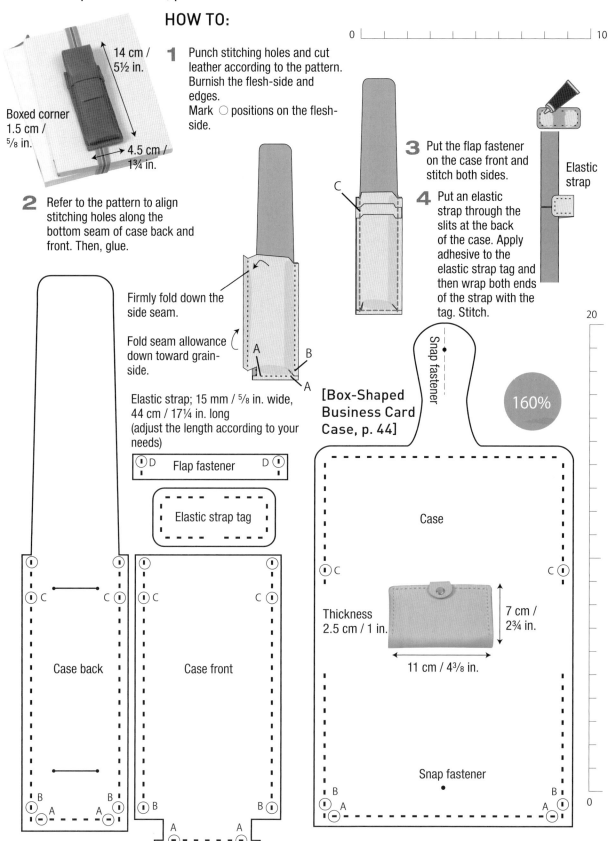

0 |⎵⎵⎵⎵⎵⎵⎵⎵⎵⎵| 10

14 cm / 5½ in.

Boxed corner 1.5 cm / ⅝ in.

4.5 cm / 1¾ in.

1 Punch stitching holes and cut leather according to the pattern. Burnish the flesh-side and edges. Mark ○ positions on the flesh-side.

3 Put the flap fastener on the case front and stitch both sides.

C

Elastic strap

4 Put an elastic strap through the slits at the back of the case. Apply adhesive to the elastic strap tag and then wrap both ends of the strap with the tag. Stitch.

2 Refer to the pattern to align stitching holes along the bottom seam of case back and front. Then, glue.

Firmly fold down the side seam.

Fold seam allowance down toward grain-side.

A   B

A

Elastic strap; 15 mm / ⅝ in. wide, 44 cm / 17¼ in. long (adjust the length according to your needs)

D   Flap fastener   D

Elastic strap tag

[Box-Shaped Business Card Case, p. 44]

Snap fastener

160%

20

Case

C   C

Thickness 2.5 cm / 1 in.

7 cm / 2¾ in.

11 cm / 4⅜ in.

C   C

Case back

Case front

B   B
A   A

B   B
A   A

A   A

B   B
A   A

Snap fastener

0

162

[Box-Shaped Business Card Case, p. 44]

HOW TO:

The method for attaching boxed-corner Pocket **1** to the case is the same as for the Box-Shaped Pen Case. Refer to p. 162.

1 Punch stitching holes and cut leather according to the pattern. Then, stitch.
Burnish the flesh-side and edges.
Mark ○ positions on the flesh-side.

2 Attach a snap fastener to the case. Refer to p. 79.

3 Glue bottom of pocket **2** and main body while referencing the pattern. Align the stitching holes and then glue.
Moisten pocket **2** leather. Then, fold the box corners and seam allowance and glue.
Stitch pocket **2** circumference.

4 Align case body and pocket **1** with the stitching holes and glue. Then, stitch.

20

Sam Browne stud

[Box-Shaped Smartphone Holder, p. 45]

See p. 164 for instructions

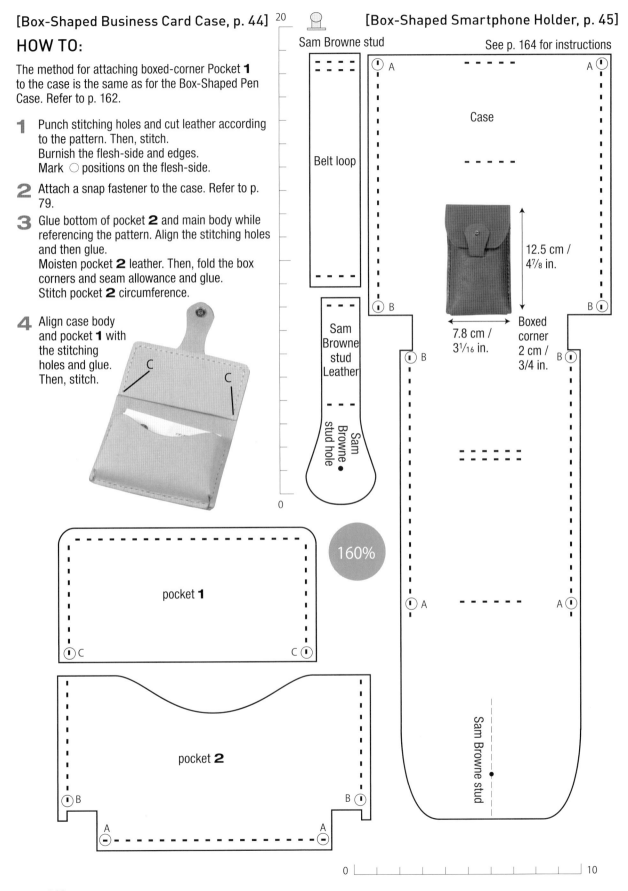

12.5 cm / 4⅞ in.

7.8 cm / 3¹/₁₆ in.

Boxed corner 2 cm / 3/4 in.

160%

0 | | | | | | | | | | 10

[Box-Shaped Smartphone Holder, p. 45]

0 |_____| 10

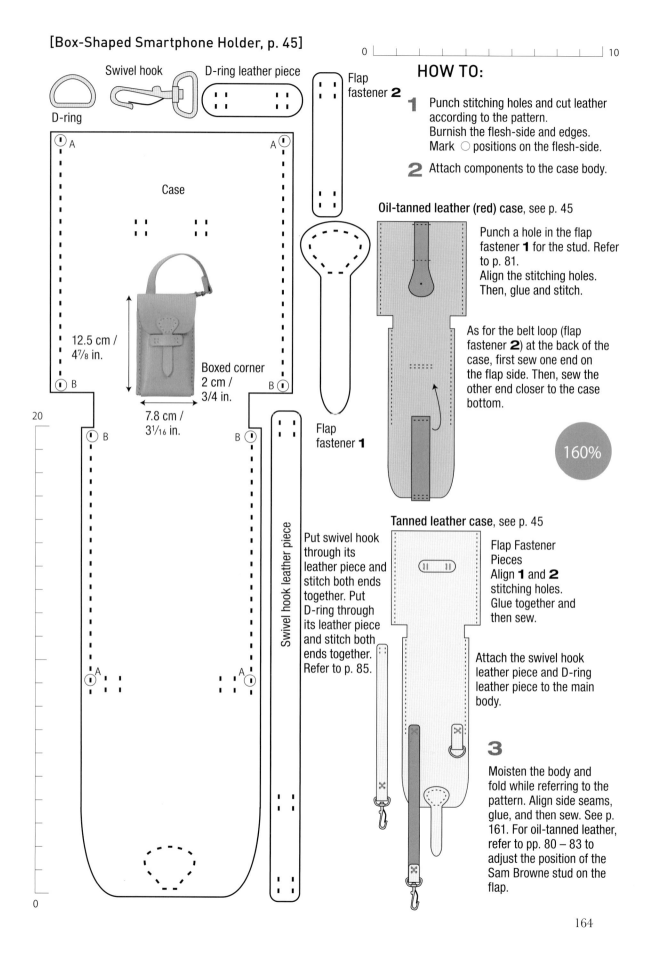

D-ring

Swivel hook

D-ring leather piece

Flap fastener 2

Case

12.5 cm / 4⅞ in.

Boxed corner 2 cm / ¾ in.

7.8 cm / 3¹/₁₆ in.

20

Swivel hook leather piece

Flap fastener 1

Put swivel hook through its leather piece and stitch both ends together. Put D-ring through its leather piece and stitch both ends together. Refer to p. 85.

0

HOW TO:

1 Punch stitching holes and cut leather according to the pattern.
Burnish the flesh-side and edges.
Mark ○ positions on the flesh-side.

2 Attach components to the case body.

Oil-tanned leather (red) case, see p. 45

Punch a hole in the flap fastener **1** for the stud. Refer to p. 81.
Align the stitching holes.
Then, glue and stitch.

As for the belt loop (flap fastener **2**) at the back of the case, first sew one end on the flap side. Then, sew the other end closer to the case bottom.

160%

Tanned leather case, see p. 45

Flap Fastener Pieces
Align **1** and **2** stitching holes.
Glue together and then sew.

Attach the swivel hook leather piece and D-ring leather piece to the main body.

3

Moisten the body and fold while referring to the pattern. Align side seams, glue, and then sew. See p. 161. For oil-tanned leather, refer to pp. 80 – 83 to adjust the position of the Sam Browne stud on the flap.

164

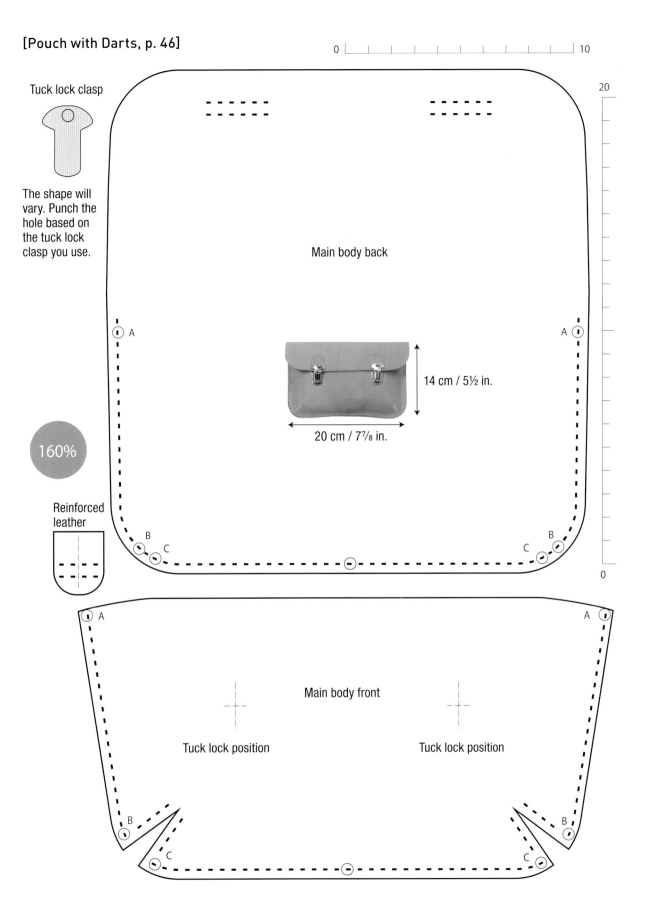

Tuck lock clasp

The shape will vary. Punch the hole based on the tuck lock clasp you use.

160%

Reinforced leather

Main body back

14 cm / 5½ in.

20 cm / 7⅞ in.

A

A

B
C

C
B

A

A

Main body front

Tuck lock position

Tuck lock position

B

C

C

B

0   10

20

0

165

[Glasses Case, p. 48]

HOW TO:

0 └───┴───┴───┴───┴───┴───┴───┴───┴───┴───┘ 10

1 Punch stitching holes and cut leather according to the pattern.
Burnish the flesh-side and edges.
Mark ○ positions on the flesh-side.

2 While keeping the bridge support piece bent, align the main body stitching holes. Glue together and then sew.

3 Fold main body, bend the leather, align stitching holes, glue, and sew.

160%

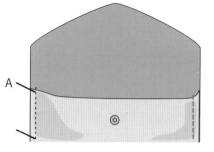

A

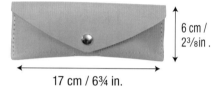

4 Insert glasses to determine position of snap fastener on the flap. Refer to p. 83. Then, attach the snap fastener.

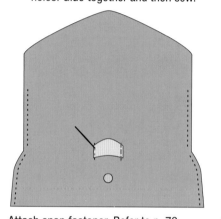

Attach snap fastener. Refer to p. 79.

6 cm /
2³/₈in .

17 cm / 6¾ in.

Bridge support

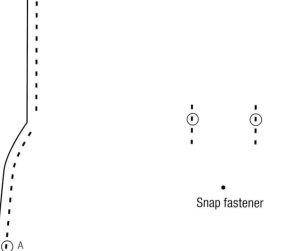

• Snap fastener

○ A   A ○

○   ○

•
Snap fastener

○ A   A ○

0 |___|___|___|___|___|___|___|___|___|___| 10

HOW TO:

1 Punch stitching holes and cut leather according to the pattern.
Burnish the flesh side and edges.
Mark ○ positions on the flesh side.

2 Attach a snap fastener on one side. See p. 79. Fold the gathers at side of main body. Sew together while aligning stitching holes.

3 Refer to the pattern. Align stitching holes on main body, glue, and sew the sides.

4 After putting something inside, refer to p. 83 to help determine the position of the snap fastener on the flap. Attach.

Snap fastener

A

A

160%

A

Snap fastener

20

8.5 cm / 3⅜ in.

13.5 cm / 5¼ in.

0

167

[Boxed-Corner Small Pouch (Bottom), p. 49]

0 |___|___|___|___|___|___|___|___|___|___| 10

HOW TO:

1 Punch stitching holes and cut leather according to the pattern.
Burnish the flesh-side and edges.
Mark ○ positions on the flesh-side.

8 cm / 3⅛ in.

14.5 cm / 5¾ in.

2 Attach a snap fastener on the main body. See p. 79.
Fold main body, bend leather, align stitching holes, and sew all the way around.

A

Swivel hook leather piece
16 – 18 cm / 6¼ – 7⅛ in. long

3 After putting something inside, refer to p. 83 to help determine the position of the snap fastener on the flap. Attach.

20

[Plastic Bottle Holder, p. 50]

Snap fastener

D-ring leather piece

160%

A

A

Main body

A   A

A   A

0

168

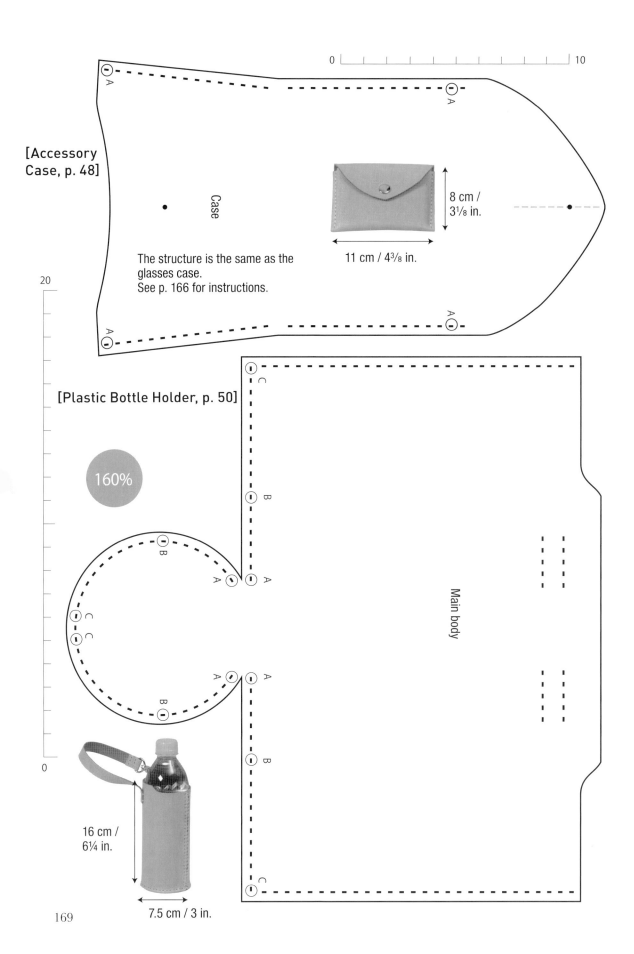

[Accessory Case, p. 48]

Case

The structure is the same as the glasses case.
See p. 166 for instructions.

8 cm / 3⅛ in.

11 cm / 4⅜ in.

[Plastic Bottle Holder, p. 50]

160%

Main body

16 cm / 6¼ in.

7.5 cm / 3 in.

0 _____ 10

20

0

["Various Types of Tanned Leather"
Drawstring Pouch, p. 54]

160%

0 |———|———|———|———|———| 10

Each cord: 5 mm / ¼ in. wide,
55 cm / 21⅝ in. long

Grommet hole

Grommet hole size 5 mm / ¼ in.

Main body, 2 Pieces

Thick cow leather	Other types of leather
Cord fastener	Cord fastener

HOW TO:

1 Punch stitching holes and cut leather according to the pattern.
Burnish the flesh-side and edges.
Mark ○ positions on the flesh-side.

2 Overlap the main body, align stitching holes, glue, and sew.

20

3 Fold and sew the cord fastener.

4 Pass the cord through the hole in the main body. Tie cord tips.

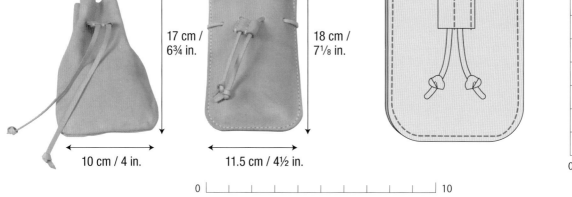

17 cm / 6¾ in.

18 cm / 7⅛ in.

10 cm / 4 in.

11.5 cm / 4½ in.

0 |———|———|———|———|———| 10

0

["Dyeing with Liquid Dye" Name Tag, p. 56]

Leather thickness = 1.4 mm / $^1/_{16}$ in.

HOW TO:

1 Punch stitching holes and cut leather according to the pattern.
Burnish the flesh-side and edges.
Mark ○ positions on the flesh-side.

160%

Front | Back

Do not cut a central window in the back

Name tag **1**

Front, 1 Piece
Back, 1 Piece

2 Overlap the main body, align stitching holes, glue, and sew.

3 Attach a snap fastener to one side of the strap. See p. 79.

Name tag **2**

Front, 1 Piece
Back, 1 Piece

4 Pass strap through main body and attach a snap fastener to the other end.

20

6 cm / 2³/₈ in.

6 cm / 2³/₈ in.

7.5 cm / 3 in.

7.5 cm / 3 in.

Name tag **3**

Front, 1 Piece
Back, 1 Piece

10.5 cm / 4¹/₈ in.

6 cm / 2³/₈ in.

7.5 cm / 3 in.

7.5 cm / 3 in.

Name tag **4**

Front, 1 Piece
Back, 1 Piece

• Snap fastener   Strap **12**   Snap fastener •

• Snap fastener   Strap **23**   Snap fastener •

0

0   10

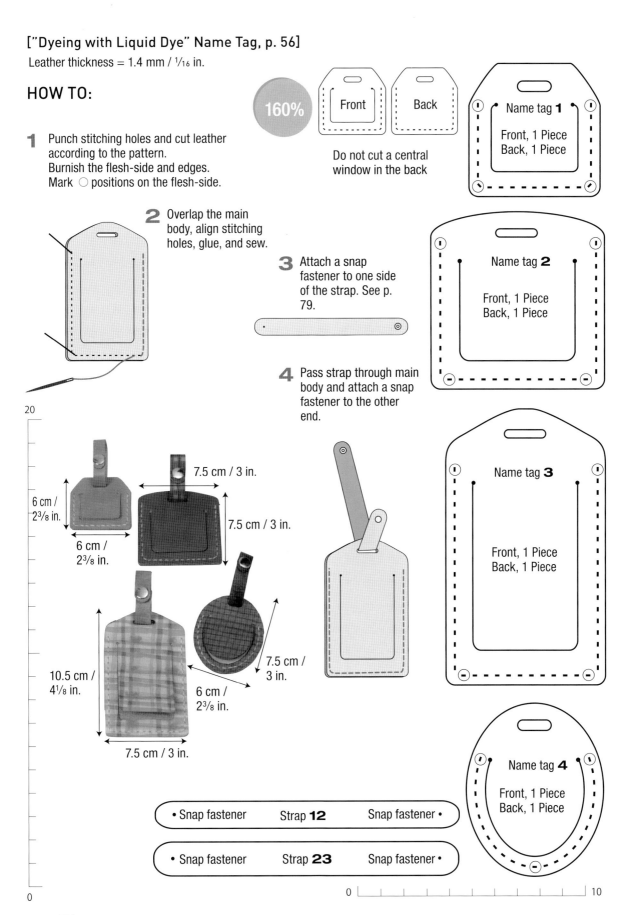

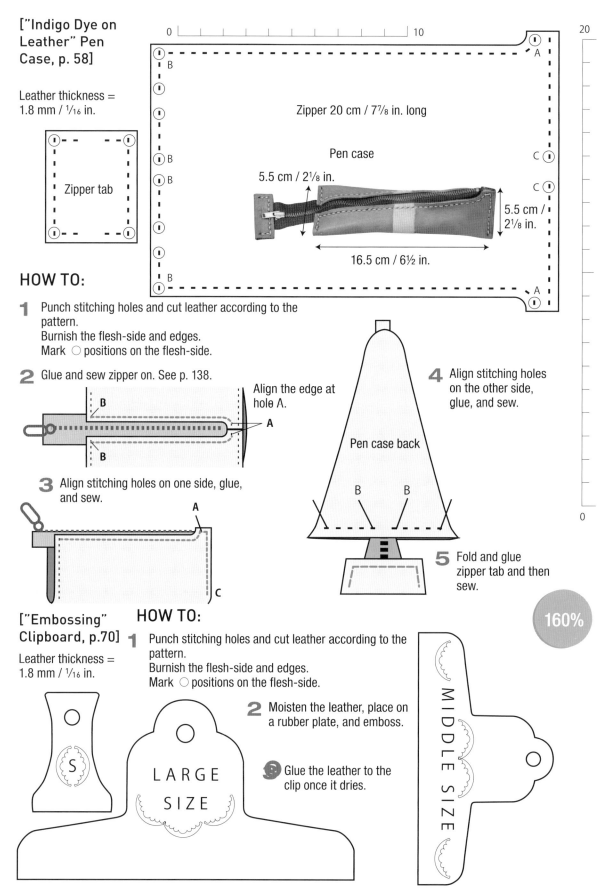

["Indigo Dye on Leather" Pen Case, p. 58]

Leather thickness = 1.8 mm / 1/16 in.

Zipper tab

0   10   20

B
A

Zipper 20 cm / 7⅞ in. long

Pen case

C

C

5.5 cm / 2⅛ in.

5.5 cm / 2⅛ in.

B
B

16.5 cm / 6½ in.

B

A

HOW TO:

1 Punch stitching holes and cut leather according to the pattern.
Burnish the flesh-side and edges.
Mark ○ positions on the flesh-side.

2 Glue and sew zipper on. See p. 138.

Align the edge at hole A.

B

A

B

3 Align stitching holes on one side, glue, and sew.

A

C

4 Align stitching holes on the other side, glue, and sew.

Pen case back

B   B

5 Fold and glue zipper tab and then sew.

160%

["Embossing" Clipboard, p.70]

Leather thickness = 1.8 mm / 1/16 in.

HOW TO:

1 Punch stitching holes and cut leather according to the pattern.
Burnish the flesh-side and edges.
Mark ○ positions on the flesh-side.

2 Moisten the leather, place on a rubber plate, and emboss.

3 Glue the leather to the clip once it dries.

S

LARGE SIZE

MIDDLE SIZE

172

Charm

["Dyeing with Markers"
Charm, p. 66]

Leather thickness =
1.8 mm / 1/16 in. thickness

Charm

Charm

Charm

Backing leather

Backing
leather

Backing
leather

["Edge Dyeing" Key
Chain, p. 68]

Leather thickness =
1.8 mm / 1/16 in.

Cut out letters one by one,
apply color to the cut sides.

1 Cut out the
contoured pieces
of leather seen on
p. 66.

HOW TO:

2 Glue
backing
leather on
the flesh-
side.

3 Place on flesh-side
of another piece
of leather and cut
along the outline.

Backing
leather

Make a hole for
a cord.

A

0

160%

["Stenciling" Flat
Pouch, p. 71]

Leather = 1.8 mm / 1/16 in.
thickness

See p. 152 for instructions.

Zipper stitching end

Flat Pouch
p. 71, bottom photo
2 pieces
Zipper 17 cm / 6⅝ in. long

0   10

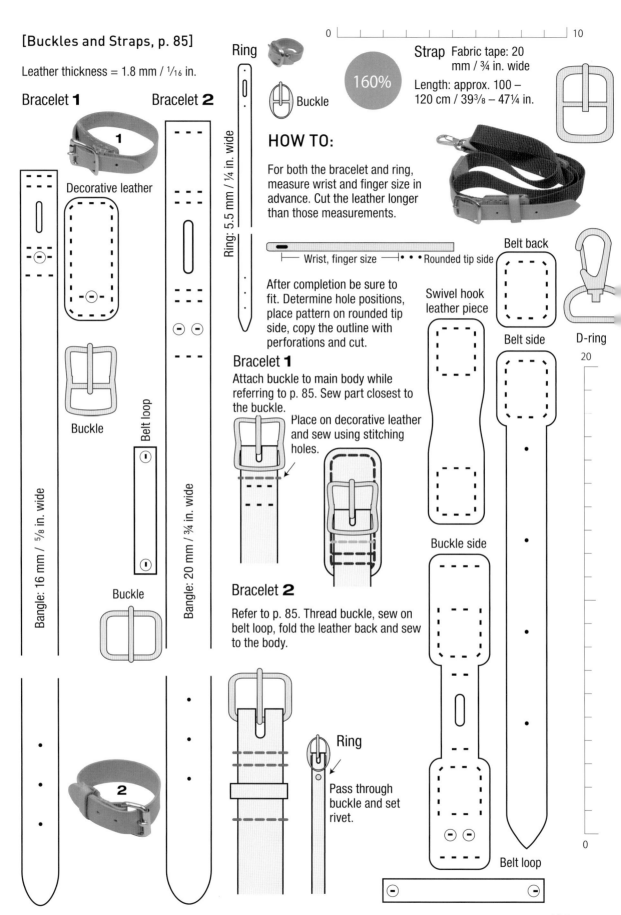

[Buckles and Straps, p. 85]

Leather thickness = 1.8 mm / 1/16 in.

Bracelet 1

Bracelet 2

Decorative leather

Buckle

Belt loop

Buckle

Bangle: 16 mm / 5/8 in. wide

Bangle: 20 mm / 3/4 in. wide

Ring: 5.5 mm / 1/4 in. wide

Ring

Buckle

160%

Strap
Fabric tape: 20 mm / 3/4 in. wide

Length: approx. 100 – 120 cm / 39 3/8 – 47 1/4 in.

HOW TO:

For both the bracelet and ring, measure wrist and finger size in advance. Cut the leather longer than those measurements.

⊢ Wrist, finger size ⊣ • • Rounded tip side

After completion be sure to fit. Determine hole positions, place pattern on rounded tip side, copy the outline with perforations and cut.

Bracelet 1

Attach buckle to main body while referring to p. 85. Sew part closest to the buckle.

Place on decorative leather and sew using stitching holes.

Bracelet 2

Refer to p. 85. Thread buckle, sew on belt loop, fold the leather back and sew to the body.

Ring

Pass through buckle and set rivet.

Belt back

Swivel hook leather piece

Belt side

D-ring

Buckle side

Belt loop

[Binoculars Case, p. 88]

Leather cord: approx. 4 mm / ⅛ in. wide,
approx. 130 – 140 cm / 51⅛ – 55⅛ in. long

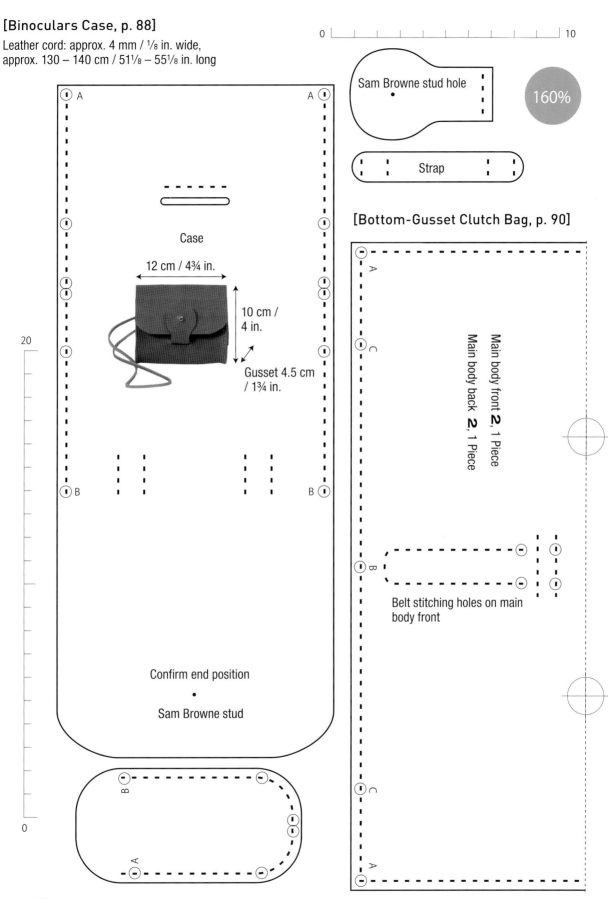

0 |__|__|__|__|__|__|__|__|__|__| 10

160%

A   A

Case

12 cm / 4¾ in.

10 cm / 4 in.

Gusset 4.5 cm / 1¾ in.

20

B   B

Confirm end position

•

Sam Browne stud

0

Sam Browne stud hole

•

Strap

[Bottom-Gusset Clutch Bag, p. 90]

A

C

Main body front **2**, 1 Piece

Main body back **2**, 1 Piece

B

Belt stitching holes on main body front

C

A

B

A

0 |⌐ ⌐ ⌐ ⌐ ⌐ ⌐ ⌐ ⌐ ⌐ ⌐ 10

Roller buckle

Belt on main body back

Belt on main body front

Main body front **1**, 1 Piece

Main body back **1**, 1 Piece

160%

Belt stitching holes on main body back

Align main body **1** and **2** using marks. Paste to a large piece of paper. Make 2 Pieces

27.5 cm / 10⅞ in.

18 cm / 7⅛ in.

7 cm / 2¾ in.

Main body front

Main body back

The front and back of the main body are the same size.
Both belt stitching holes are marked on the pattern. Punch only the indicated stitching holes.

C   B   C

A   A

Bag bottom

C   B   C

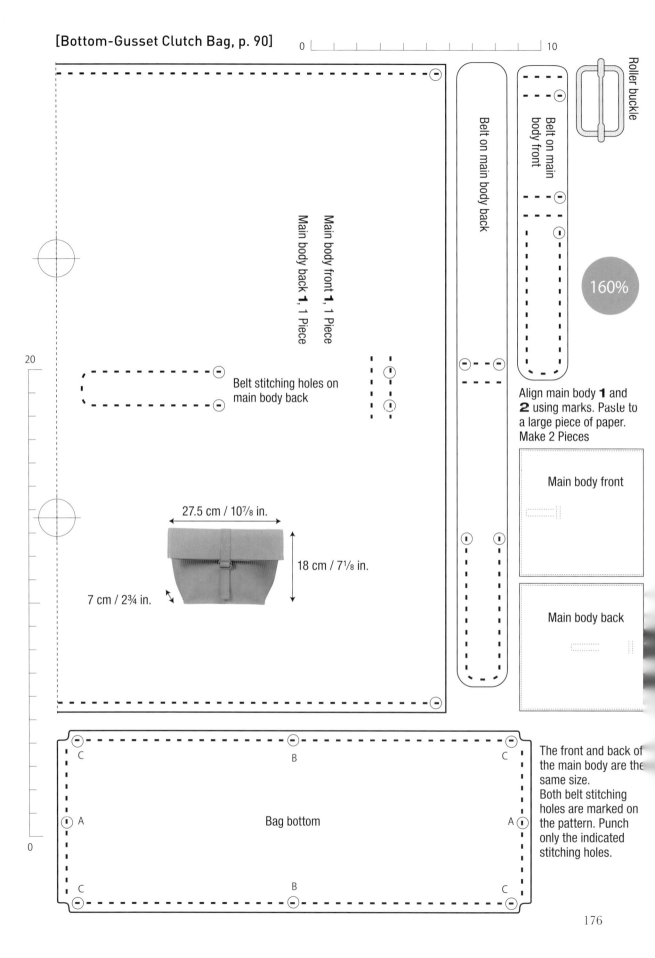

[Bicolor Tote Bag, p. 92]

160%

0 | | | | | | | | | | | 10

F

E   E

C   C
C   C

Bag bottom

Handle on main body, 4 Pieces

G

33 cm / 13 in.

24 cm / 9½ in.

11 cm / 4³⁄₈ in.

C   C
C   C

E   E

F

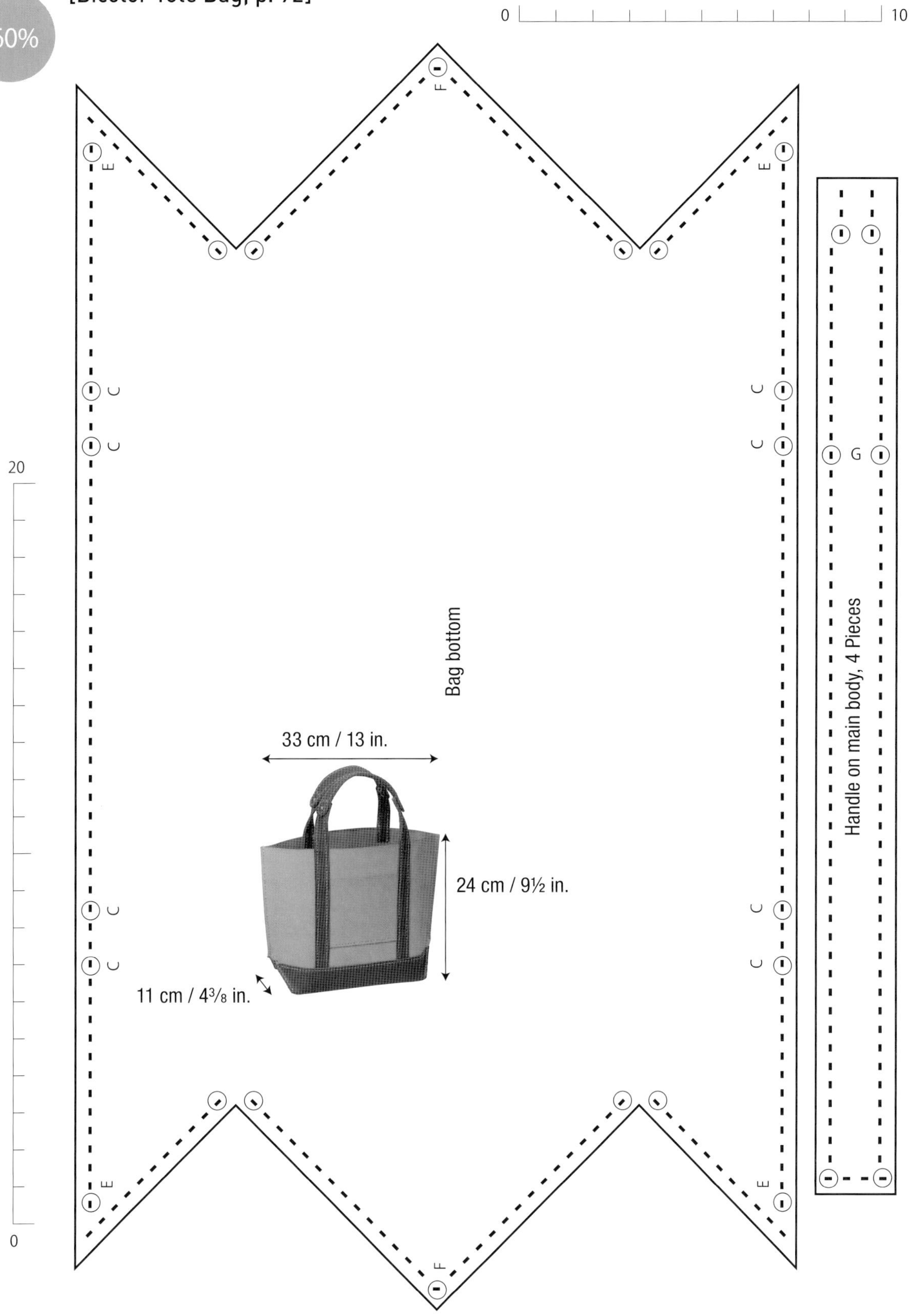

160%

0 |___|___|___|___|___|___|___|___|___|___| 10

The front and back of
the main body are the
same size.
Stitching holes for the
pocket are only made
on the front of the main
body.

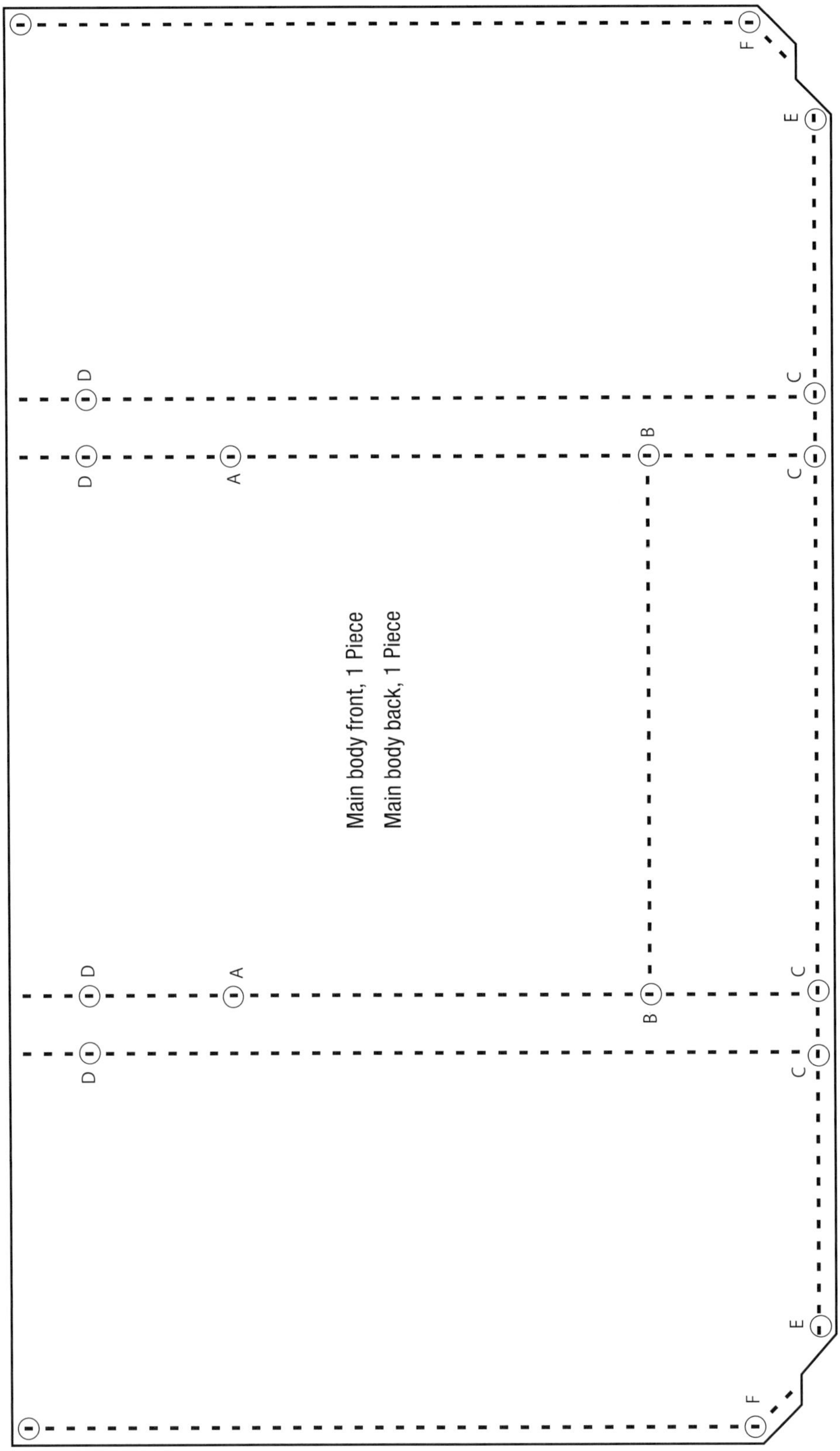

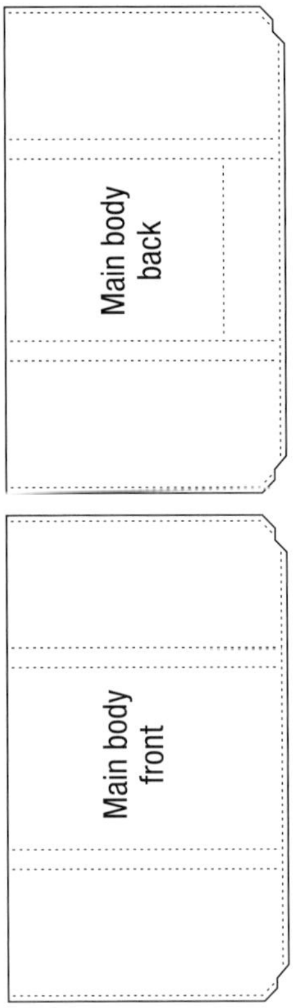

F

E

D

D

A

B

C

C

20

Main body front, 1 Piece
Main body back, 1 Piece

Main body
back

Main body
front

D

A

B

C

D

C

E

F

0

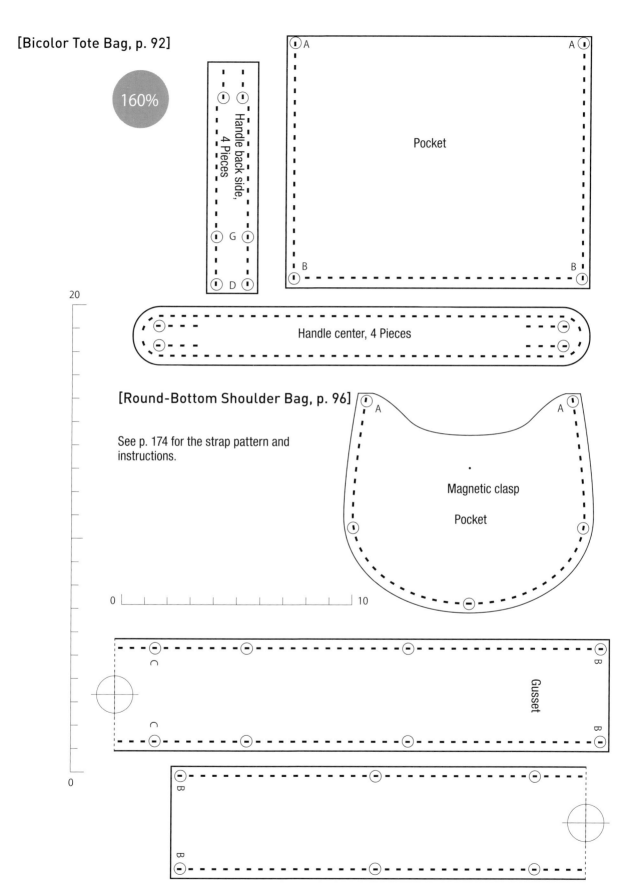

[Bicolor Tote Bag, p. 92]

160%

Handle back side, 4 Pieces

G

D

Pocket

A   A

B   B

Handle center, 4 Pieces

[Round-Bottom Shoulder Bag, p. 96]

See p. 174 for the strap pattern and instructions.

A   A

Magnetic clasp

Pocket

20

0   10

0

Gusset

C

C

B

B

B

B

179

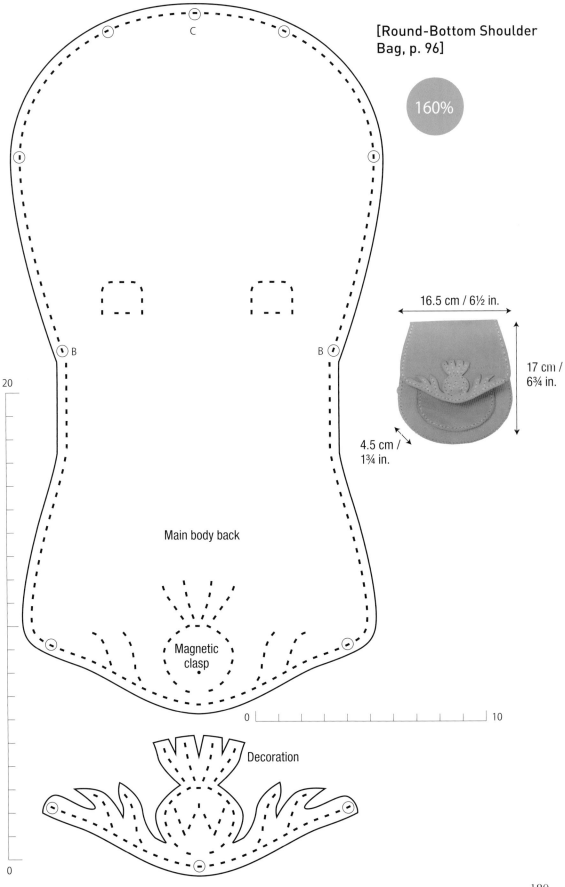

[Round-Bottom Shoulder Bag, p. 96]

160%

C

B

B

20

16.5 cm / 6½ in.

17 cm / 6¾ in.

4.5 cm / 1¾ in.

Main body back

Magnetic clasp

0   10

Decoration

0

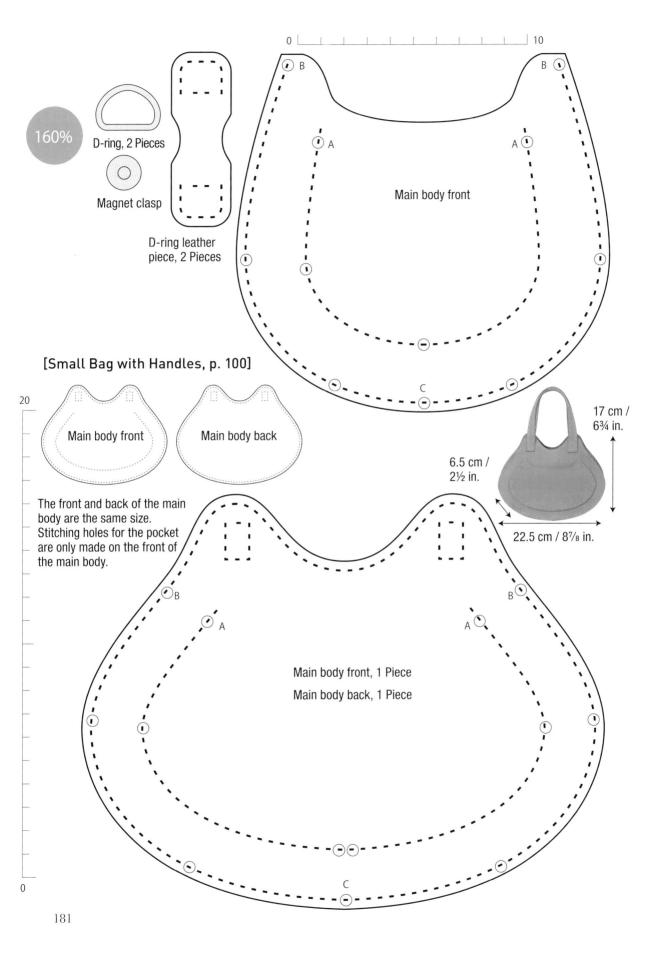

160%

D-ring, 2 Pieces

Magnet clasp

D-ring leather
piece, 2 Pieces

0   10

B   B

A   A

Main body front

C

[Small Bag with Handles, p. 100]

20

Main body front   Main body back

The front and back of the main
body are the same size.
Stitching holes for the pocket
are only made on the front of
the main body.

17 cm /
6¾ in.

6.5 cm /
2½ in.

22.5 cm / 8⅞ in.

B   B

A   A

Main body front, 1 Piece

Main body back, 1 Piece

C

0

[Small Bag with Handles, p. 100]

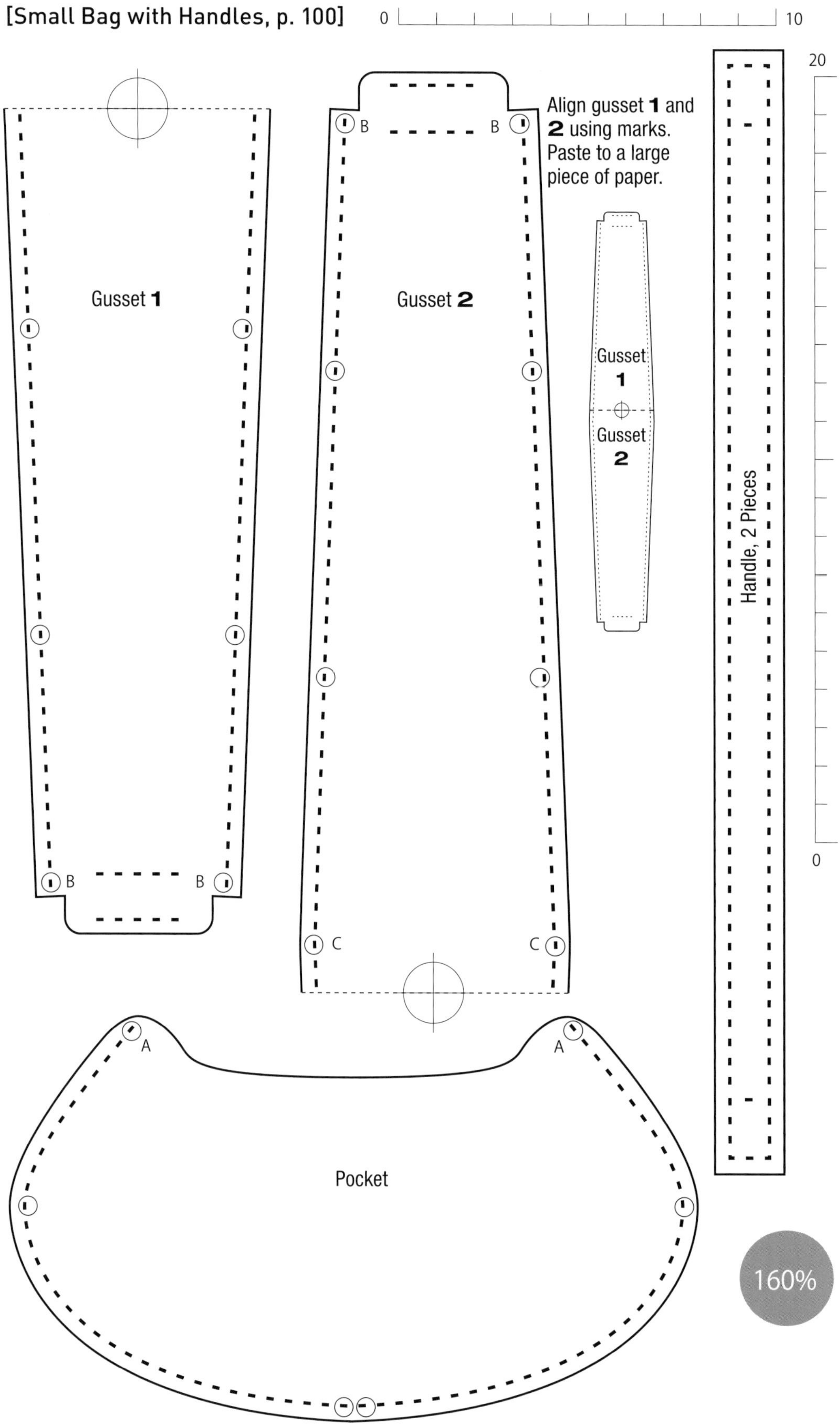

0 |___|___|___|___|___|___|___|___|___|___| 10

20

Gusset 1

Gusset 2

Align gusset **1** and **2** using marks. Paste to a large piece of paper.

B   B

Gusset
1

Gusset
2

Handle, 2 Pieces

B   B

C   C

0

A   A

Pocket

160%

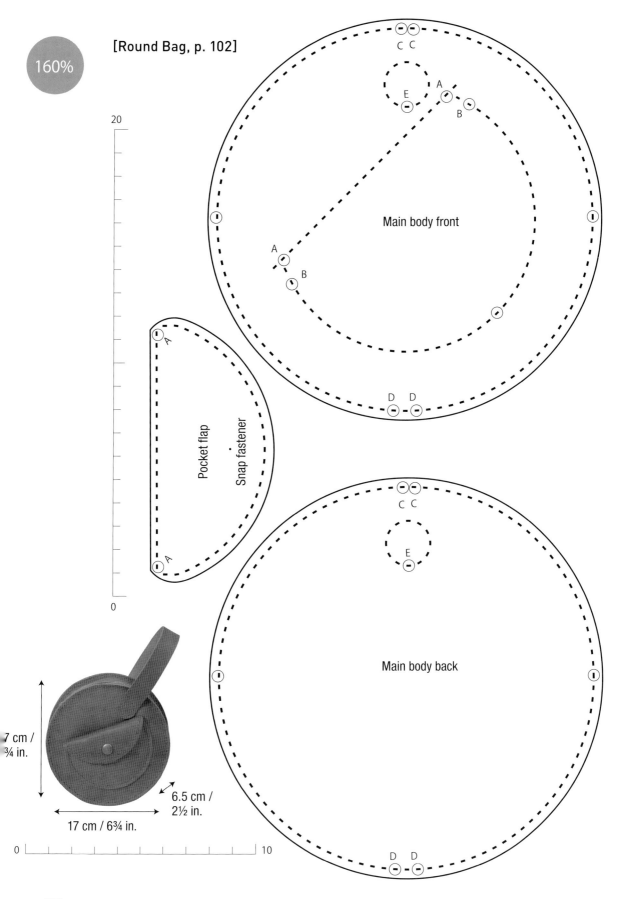

[Round Bag, p. 102]

160%

Main body front

Pocket flap
Snap fastener

Main body back

C C
E
A
B
A
B
D D
E

7 cm / ¾ in.

6.5 cm / 2½ in.

17 cm / 6¾ in.

0   10

20

0

183

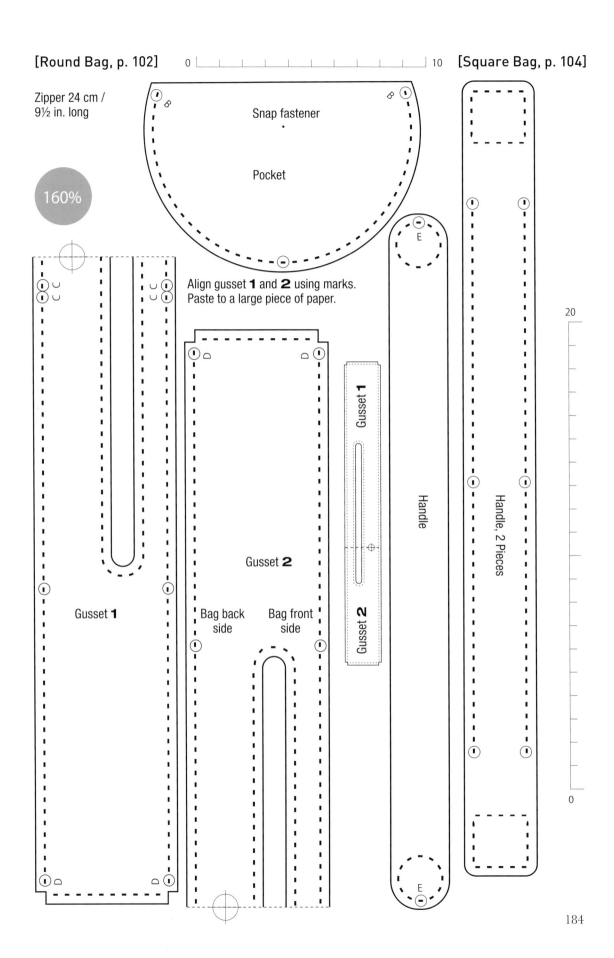

[Round Bag, p. 102]

0 |—————| 10

[Square Bag, p. 104]

Zipper 24 cm /
9½ in. long

160%

Snap fastener

Pocket

Align gusset **1** and **2** using marks.
Paste to a large piece of paper.

Gusset **1**

Gusset **2**

Bag back
side

Bag front
side

Gusset **1**

Gusset **2**

Handle

E

E

Handle, 2 Pieces

20

0

184

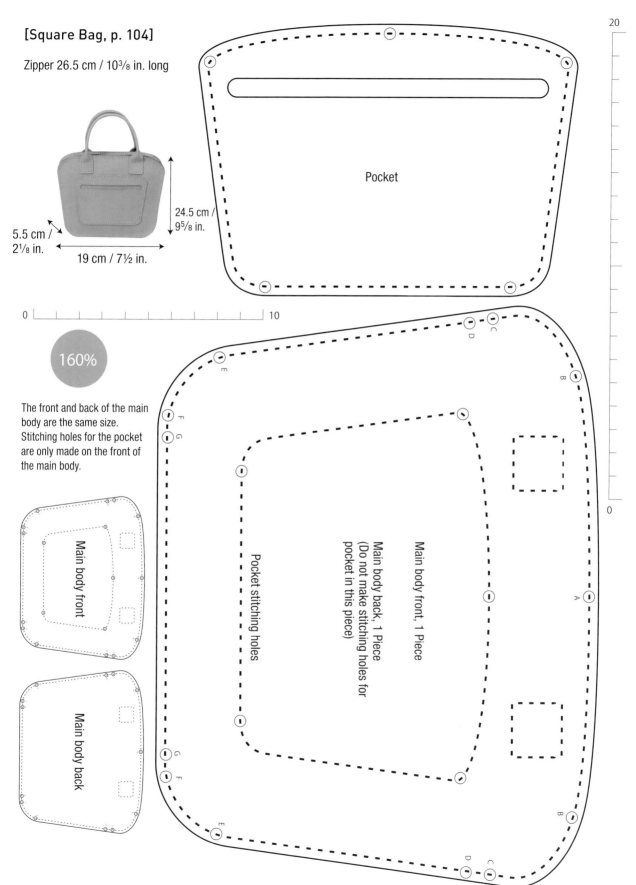

[Square Bag, p. 104]

Zipper 26.5 cm / 10³⁄₈ in. long

24.5 cm / 9⁵⁄₈ in.

5.5 cm / 2¹⁄₈ in.

19 cm / 7½ in.

160%

The front and back of the main body are the same size. Stitching holes for the pocket are only made on the front of the main body.

Pocket

Main body front

Main body back

Pocket stitching holes

Main body back, 1 Piece (Do not make stitching holes for pocket in this piece)

Main body front, 1 Piece

0 |⎯⎯⎯⎯⎯⎯⎯⎯⎯⎯⎯⎯⎯⎯| 10

160%

[Square Bag, p. 104]

D | D

Side gusset, 2 Pieces

E | E

F | F

G | G

Bottom gusset, 2 Pieces

G | G

C — Top gusset — C

B | B

26.5 cm / 10³/₈ in.

A | A

B | B

C | C

[Satchel-Style Bag, p. 108]

A | A

See p. 174 for the strap pattern and instructions

Pocket gusset

B | B
B | B

A | A

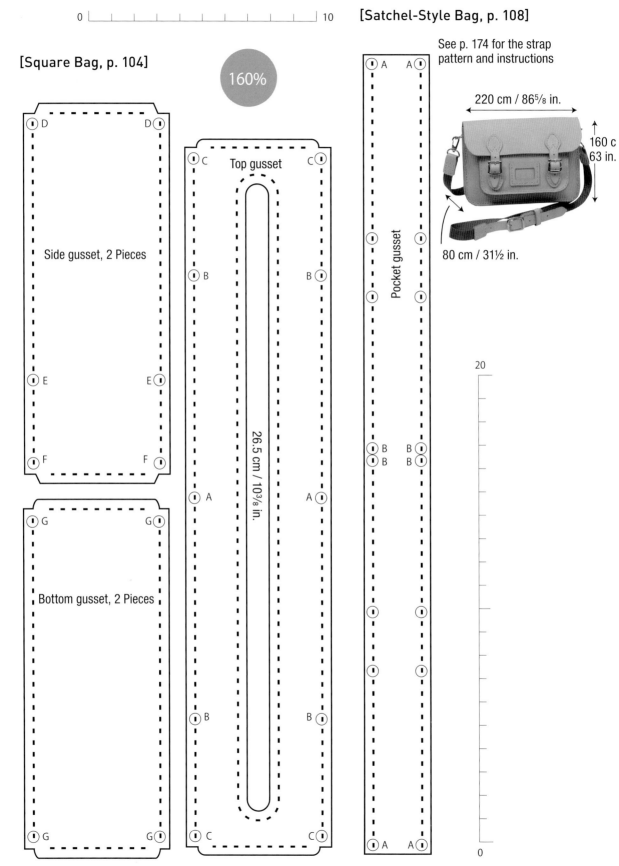

220 cm / 86⁵/₈ in.

160 c
63 in.

80 cm / 31½ in.

20

0

160%

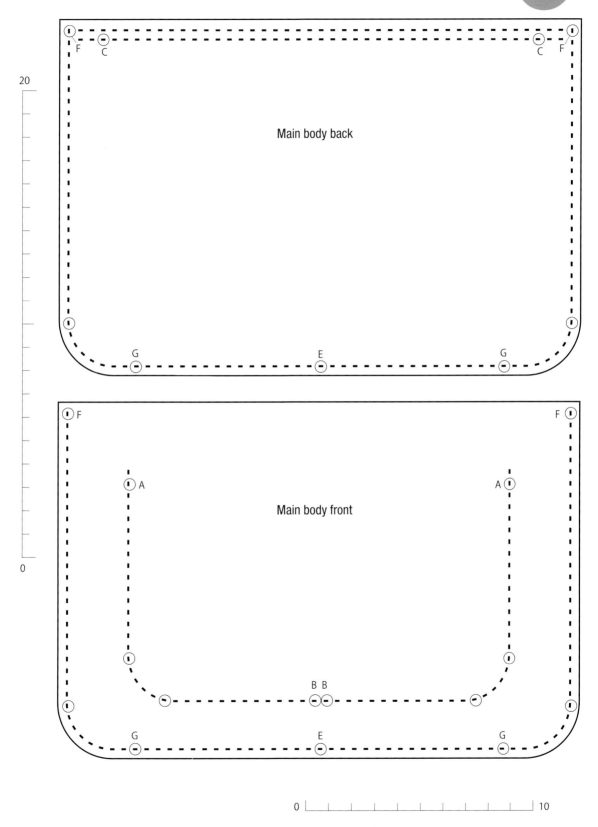

Main body back

Main body front

20

0

0   10

[Satchel-Style Bag, p. 108]

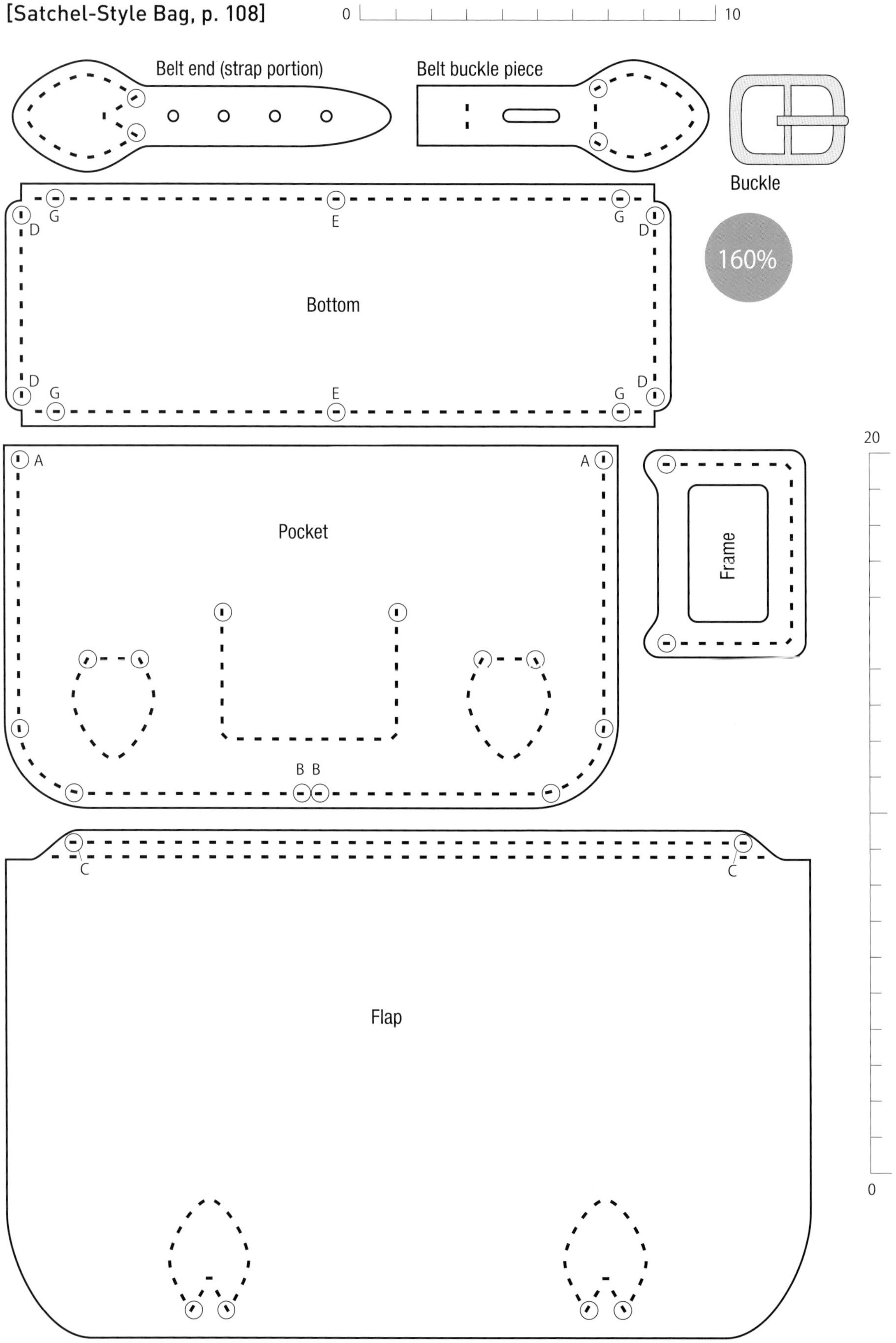

0
10
Belt end (strap portion)
Belt buckle piece
Buckle
160%
G
E
G
D
D
Bottom
D
G
E
G
D
A
A
Pocket
Frame
B B
20
0
C
C
Flap

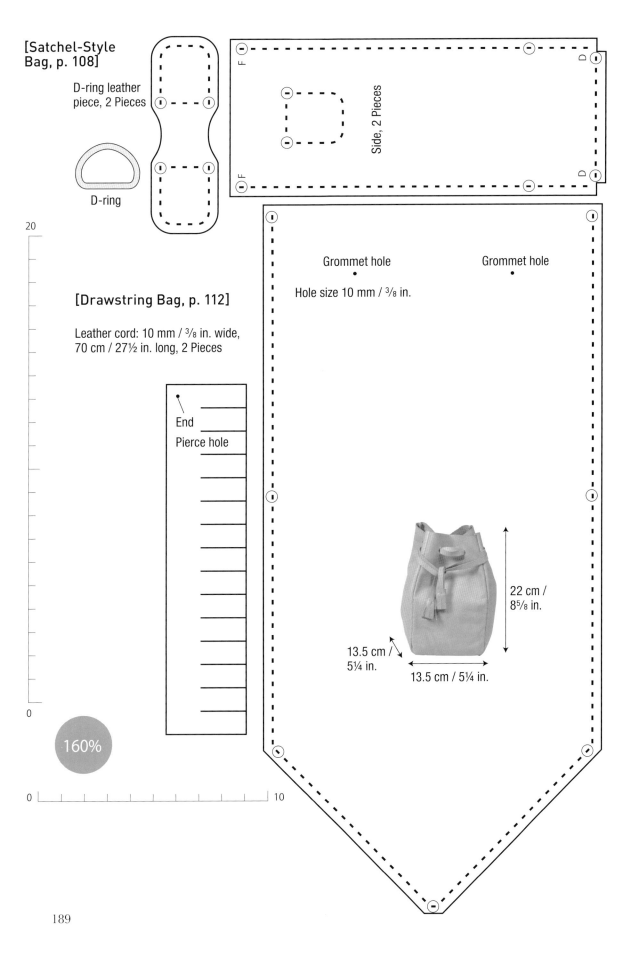

[Satchel-Style Bag, p. 108]

D-ring leather piece, 2 Pieces

D-ring

Side, 2 Pieces

[Drawstring Bag, p. 112]

Leather cord: 10 mm / ³⁄₈ in. wide, 70 cm / 27½ in. long, 2 Pieces

Grommet hole   Grommet hole

Hole size 10 mm / ³⁄₈ in.

End

Pierce hole

160%

22 cm / 8⁵⁄₈ in.

13.5 cm / 5¼ in.

13.5 cm / 5¼ in.

20

0

0   10

HOW TO:

Needle Case

Wax Block Case

160%

1

Punch stitching holes and cut leather according to the pattern. Burnish the flesh-side and edges.
Mark ○ positions on the flesh-side.

2

While referring to the pattern, sew the handles together using stitching holes.

3

Attach a snap fastener to the case. See p. 79.

4

Sew pincushion **1** and **2** together using stitching holes.

5

Fold the case body, insert pincushion, align stitching holes, and sew.

6

Set needles on pincushion, but before attaching the snap fastener, check the position on the flap side. See p. 83. Needles come in a variety of sizes, from very long to short. If you want to use long needles, you must cut out the pattern and adjust the length of the flap based on the needle size.

A

B

Wax Block Case

1

Prepare leather the same as for the needle case.

2

Refer to the pattern and sew the handle together using stitching holes. Attach a snap fastener to the case body. See p. 79.

3

For the snap fastener on the flap side, insert the wax and check the position of the snap fastener before attaching. Refer to p. 83.

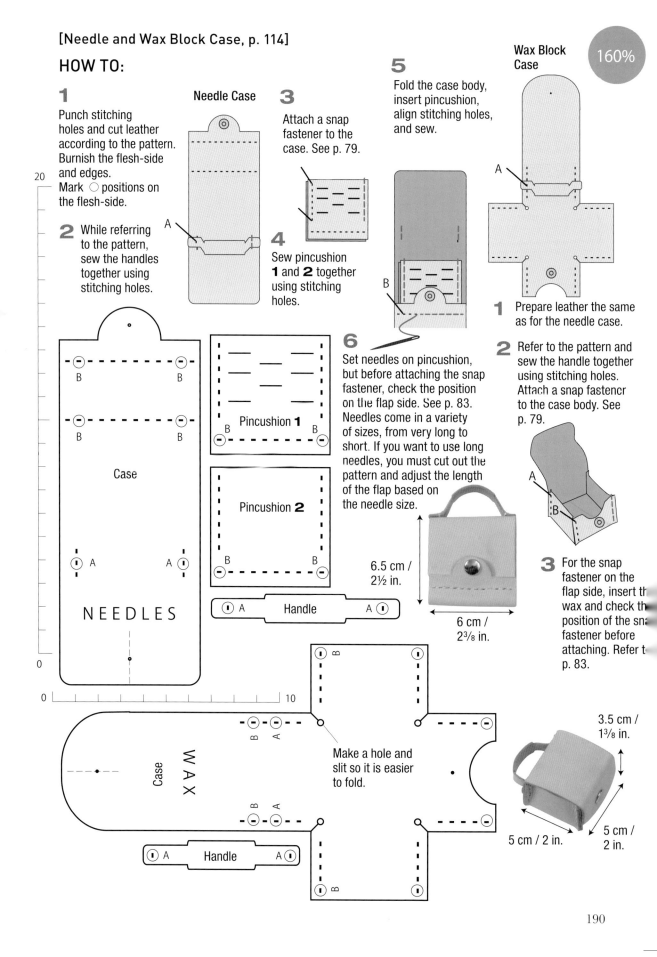

Case

B B

B B

A A

NEEDLES

Pincushion **1**

B B

B B

Pincushion **2**

B B

B B

A Handle A

6.5 cm / 2½ in.

6 cm / 2³⁄₈ in.

Case WAX

B A

Make a hole and slit so it is easier to fold.

B A

B

B

A Handle A

3.5 cm / 1³⁄₈ in.

5 cm / 2 in.

5 cm / 2 in.

20

0

0 ———————— 10

[Leather Fortune Cookie, p. 5]

HOW TO:

1 Cut leather according to the pattern. Burnish the flesh-side and edges.

2 Bend the body while referencing p. 5. Once dry, glue around the main body and sandwich tag to bond it. Make a hole with a single-hole punch.

★ Since this piece has been moistened to form its shape, it will deform if it gets wet. It is best to just use this piece as a decoration as it is not very durable.

160%

Tag

Body

12 cm / 4¾ in.

5.5 cm / 2⅛ in.

Once in a while, even though you think that you made sure to align the stitching holes for gluing, you may notice that the number of holes doesn't match. Use the following method to adjust the stitching holes. The finished shape is a bit warped, so we must moisten the leather. This will stretch out the leather and allow the shape to adjust.

When the Stitching Holes Are Misaligned

[Peeling Off Glued Areas]

Force the scratch awl in a gap at the glued edge. Pry open the glued area as you move the scratch awl around at an angle.

Edge

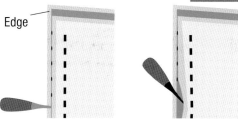

[When an Edge Does Not Align]

When top edge of the leather doesn't align for some reason, peel off the glued seam allowance about 10 cm (approx. 4 in.) down from the top edge. Moisten the shorter leather and stretch. After the moistened leather has dried, add one hole by piercing a lacing needle through the leather.

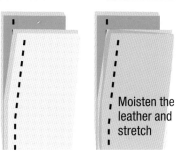

Moisten the leather and stretch

[Sew While Aligning Holes]

Stop stitching a few stitches before where the stitching hole was added. Then, start stitching from the top edge and use a scratch awl to align the perforations.

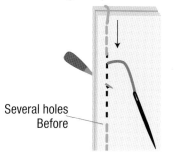

Several holes Before

After sewing for a few holes, open the seam allowance, apply glue, and bond firmly.

Use a scratch awl, etc., to apply glue to inside of the seam.

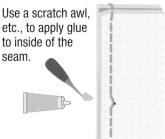

[If the Stitching Holes Don't Meet Up in the Middle]

As above, moisten and stretch, add holes, align, and then sew.

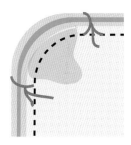

PIGPONG

http://www.sigma-pig.com/

Pigpong is Yoko Ganaha and Piggy Tsujioka's arts and crafts production firm. Product planning, book design, illustration, dyeing, creating objects, displays, etc.: Pigpong delivers unique projects full of originality.

We have taken every precaution to verify the pattern and leathercrafting process of each leather product presented; however, if you encounter any problems resulting from the pattern and leathercrafting process please let us know. That being said, the author and publisher will not be held responsible for any damage caused by construction of the pieces noted in this book.

Other Schiffer Books on Related Subjects:

Leathercraft: Traditional Handcrafted Leatherwork Skills and Projects, Nigel Armitage, ISBN 978-0-7643-6039-8

The Art of Leather Inlay and Overlay: A Guide to the Techniques for Top Results, Lisa Sorrell, ISBN 978-0-7643-5121-1

Published by Schiffer Publishing, Ltd.
4880 Lower Valley Road
Atglen, PA 19310
Phone: (610) 593-1777; Fax: (610) 593-2002
Email: Info@schifferbooks.com
Web: www.schifferbooks.com

For our complete selection of fine books on this and related subjects, please visit our website at www.schifferbooks.com. You may also write for a free catalog.

Schiffer Publishing's titles are available at special discounts for bulk purchases for sales promotions or premiums. Special editions, including personalized covers, corporate imprints, and excerpts, can be created in large quantities for special needs. For more information, contact the publisher.

We are always looking for people to write books on new and related subjects. If you have an idea for a book, please contact us at proposals@schifferbooks.com.

Numegawa Craft Handbook
© 2016 Yoko Ganaha and Piggy Tsujioka
© 2016 GRAPHIC-SHA PUBLISHING CO., LTD
This book was first designed and published in Japan in 2016 by Graphic-sha Publishing Co, Ltd.
This English edition was published in 2022 by Schiffer Publishing, Ltd.

English translation rights arranged with Graphic-sha Publishing Co, Ltd. through Japan UNI Agency, Inc., Tokyo

Original edition creative staff

Photos:	Tadashi Ikeda
Book design:	Yoko Ganaha
Creative Cooperation:	Hisako Rokkaku, Mitsue Kobayashi, Mariko Adac
Editing:	Naoko Yamamoto (Graphic-sha Publishing)
Cooperation:	SEIWA, KODOMONOKAO, TSUKINEKO, TAMURAKO-Sho

English translation:	Kevin Wilson
English edition layout:	Shinichi Ishioka
Production and Management:	Takako Motoki (Graphic-sha Publishing)